"You're Not Listening"

Baltimore Youth Speak Out

You're Not Listening
Baltimore Youth Speak Out

Anna K. Stone and Cynthia Hartzler-Miller
editors

Apprentice House
Baltimore, Maryland

Copyright © 2010 Anna K. Stone and Cynthia Hartzler-Miller

All rights reserved. No part of this book may be reproduced or transmitted in any form or by any means, electronic or mechanical, including photocopy, recording, or any information storage and retrieval system, without prior permission from the publisher (except by reviewers who may quote brief passages).

ISBN: 978-1-934074-56-5

Printed in the United States of America

First Edition

Published by Apprentice House
The Future of Publishing…Today!

Apprentice House
Communication Department
Loyola University Maryland
4501 N. Charles Street
Baltimore, MD 21210

410.617.5265
www.ApprenticeHouse.com
info@ApprenticeHouse.com

*The editors wish to thank several people
who made this book possible.*

> Mrs. Denise Gordon for creating time and space for Southside students to work on their book.
>
> Ms. LaShaviar Burns and Mrs. Marcia Grove for alerting students about meetings and deadlines.
>
> Dr. Edwin T. Johnson for his valuable contributions to the introductory chapter.
>
> Mrs. Dawn Converse of Word Processing Unlimited for her careful and eager attention to our students' words.
>
> All of the students and staff at Apprentice House for believing in this project.

And most notably…

> The thirty-four marvelous young people who revealed their lives, ideas and dreams for the world to see, critique, embrace, distort and cultivate.

Thank you for your courage.

INTRODUCTION

1
Parents and Family

Janae: When you tell somebody "don't," don't you know that's going to make somebody want to do it more?

2
Teachers and School

Aaron S.: School is for when you go there you got a second mother or second father.

3
Friends and Enemies

Deinera: The thing I didn't like about school was the peers. I'm not saying they was the reason I slacked, but by me knowing everybody, by being well known, they was just a huge distraction.

4
Identity and Interests

Ashley: You gotta love yourself, no matter what. You might not have no hair. You still gotta love yourself.

5
Sex and Marriage

Deloris: Boys stink. All of them are losers. All of them trifling. They all got kids or they're just trifling, want to play everybody. I'll probably get married, but not right now.

6
Career and Future

Malcolm: If you ain't got no talent, you ain't going nowhere. And if you got no bling, you ain't going nowhere.

7
Politics and Society

Isaiah: If he gets elected, I think Barack Obama will make changes to the school. Like helping out in the schools with supplies and all that.

8
Racism and Poverty

Saraii: I think sometimes the Caucasians get the better service and better things than we do. Like you go in a county school where a lot of Caucasians are at, they got better desks, better books, newer stuff, and you come to our school and our desks are raggedy. I think even Mexicans get better service than we do.

9
Crime and Violence

Miguel: Half of the cops you see really are not from Baltimore City. The police department is getting people from New York City, Philadelphia. And their mentality is like okay, I'm going to deal with kids with smart attitudes, who mouth off. But we're really not like that.

10
Credos to Live By

Lajuane: There ain't one person that's perfect because if they was, they wouldn't be here. Here meaning earth, not just Southside.

INTRODUCTION

Images of Urban Youth

Thug, deficient, lazy, irresponsible, disadvantaged. Too often, urban youth – particularly African American youth – are portrayed as caricatures. Such labels persist in part because adults are unwilling or unable to listen to what teenagers are saying about themselves. "You're Not Listening" provides a forum for young people to tell their own stories in their own words about their own lives and in the process, challenge readers to reexamine the predispositions and stereotypes they may hold about cities and city kids.

The young people who speak out in these pages are all growing up amidst underfunded, largely segregated schools, wages that do not keep up with inflation, inadequate health care, substandard housing, and racial profiling. But urban teenagers are not monolithic in their responses to such realities. Some try harder than others to do well in school, some – but not all - work to supplement the family income, and some have strong opinions about racism and poverty, while others have little interest in discussing the subject. Like all teenagers, they must navigate the choppy waters of adolescent development: forge their own academic, career and sexual identities, establish peer relationships, and negotiate autonomy from parents. They do so in ways that resist the labels imposed by many adults, those who think they know city kids after a superficial glance. Like all teenagers, they long to be heard and understood. To read this book with an open mind is to take the risk of saying to these thirty-four young people: "I am listening."

Growing Up in Cherry Hill

You're Not Listening is a collection of first-person narratives by thirty-four Baltimore City youth, all of whom attend, left or graduated from Southside Academy, a public high school in Cherry Hill, one of Baltimore's high poverty, predominately African American neighborhoods. Some of the youth who share their stories and ideas in these pages are among Southside's highest-achievers. Their academic identities are as strong as those of students attending the private college prep schools in Baltimore's wealthiest areas. And some of our contributors are among the lowest-achievers, with spotty attendance, school suspensions, criminal arrests, or repeated transfers to and from alternative schools. Across the spectrum, all thirty-four youth have a lot on their minds and seized the opportunity to be heard.

Nationally, Cherry Hill was once identified as the largest public housing project east of Chicago (Breihan, 2002). Unlike most Baltimore neighborhoods, Cherry Hill is isolated and separated from the rest of the city by physical borders that include a river and train tracks. Only three streets allow entry into or out of the community.

The first homes built in Cherry Hill consisted of de jure segregated public housing intended for African American workers migrating to Baltimore for World War II employment opportunities. The south Baltimore site – originally zoned for industrial use as it was a mosquito-infested swamp downwind from the city incinerator - was selected by city planners after Whites vigorously opposed "Negro housing" in other parts of the city ("Pressure for better housing will continue," 1943). In the 1970s and 80s, the community's isolation intensified the effects of drug-related crime and gang activity.

Throughout the post-Brown era, few Whites attended Cherry Hill schools. Integration efforts never succeeded in creating racial balance in these neighborhood schools, a failure experienced by nearly all Baltimore City public schools (NEA, 1967). White students began attending Southside Academy in 2006 when the high school nearest to their neighborhood closed its doors as part of a city-wide plan to deal with the reduced school-age population (a result of ongoing migration by Baltimore's White and middle class residents to the suburbs). The thirty-four students whose narratives you will read in this book represent the demographics of Southside Academy: thirty-one are African American and three are Caucasian.

The legacy of racism, housing segregation and economic disinvestment in the Cherry Hill community is evident in the statistics: the population is 98 percent Black; 70 percent of the households earn an annual income of less than $25,000; and in a typical year, there are nearly 250 reports of violent crime and 1500 juvenile arrests - about 20 percent of these are drug-related (Baltimore Neighborhoods Indicator Alliance, 2007). According to a recent study by the Baltimore City Health Department (2008), Cherry Hill youth (ages 15-24) are more than twice as likely to die (and more than twice as likely to die from HIV/AIDS and homicide) than the average Baltimore teenager.

Narrative, Voice and Dialect

In 2007-2008 the editors invited Southside Academy students in Anna Stone's English classes to record their experiences, perceptions, and opinions about a range of topics: family, school, sex, identity, racism, politics, and crime. The students edited their own transcripts to produce this book. They chose the title You're Not Listening to express concern that adults don't listen closely enough to the voices of today's youth.

As editors, we sought to preserve the students' voices in each chapter, including their use of slang and dialect. We take issue with critics who argue that this kind of talk is inferior to the language of the dominant culture. Unlike many members of the dominant culture, Southside students are bilingual; they are fluent in both "standard English" and the language of their (predominately African American) communities. They typically use standard English when they are addressing individuals in positions of authority, while they speak in dialect with family and friends. This is called "code-switching," a skill that many African Americans master at an early age, because it enables cultural assimilation while maintaining one's ties to a rich heritage. The fact that Southside students chose to use dialect in their interviews for You're Not Listening suggests that they were more comfortable with us than they may have felt with strangers.

The decision to use dialect may also be linked to the desire to communicate the meanings, emotion and emphases contained within certain words and phrasings. Often meaning and emotion is conveyed not only by what is said, but also by how it is said. Consider, for example, how Tarena reacted to teachers who tell students with poor grades, "If you keep acting that way you're going to work at McDonald's:"

> Ain't nothing wrong with that. Some kids, like us aged 14 and 15, we want a job. That's the only job we can get. I can be making straight A's in school and

> if McDonald's the only job they
> hiring, that's where I'm gonna
> work. Like "she ain't go to school,
> she ain't got a diploma, look
> where she working at." That don't
> mean nothing. I could have my
> diploma, a college degree, and still
> work at McDonald's.

Tarena could have chosen to use "isn't" instead of "ain't," "anything" instead of "nothing," "going to work" instead of "gonna work" and "look where she is working" instead of "look where she working at." But it seems likely that the use of standard English in this case would have lessened the dual significance of her statement. By her choice of language, Tarena asserted resistance both against teachers who would try to impose their definitions of gainful employment as well as a dominant culture trying to impose its definition of acceptable speech.

Organization of the Book

The chapters are organized topically with Listening to … sections written by Anna Stone based on her interactions with each student both in the classroom and outside of the school setting. These sections provide context and details about each teenagers' unique and complicated life circumstances, along with Anna's insights – gleaned from her practice of carefully and compassionately observing and listening to each student, as well as her knowledge of adolescent development in general and the characteristics of race and poverty in Baltimore in particular. The conclusion chapter draws lessons learned from listening to these young people in terms of how teachers, families and public officials might respond to better meet the needs of Baltimore's urban youth. Throughout the conclusion chapter, we offer concrete advice directed at all those who interact with urban youth on a regular basis or create policies that directly impact them.

References

Baltimore City Health Department and Johns Hopkins Bloomberg School of Health (2008). Cherry Hill Health Profile 2008.[Online] Available: http://www.baltimorehealth.org/info/neighborhood/7%20Cherry%20Hill.pdf.

Baltimore Neighborhoods Indicator Alliance (2007). Vital signs IV [Online]. Available: http://www.ubalt.edu/bnia/about/index.html.

Breihan, J. R. (2002). Cherry Hill: A community history. Baltimore, MD: Loyola College. Retrieved September 24, 2009 from http://www.cherryhillnet.org/documents/Coalition/cherryhillhistory.pdf.

National Education Association (1967). Baltimore Maryland change and contrast: The children and the public schools. (Report). Washington, DC: Author.

Pressure for better housing will continue (1943, October 20). Baltimore Afro-American Newspaper.

1
PARENTS AND FAMILY

It's hard for a teenage child, being fifteen,, but I tell my mother everything and I think she knows me like a book that she read fifty times. **DEAIRRA**

Sometimes I'm like why can't we be like the Cosby's or something? Why can't we live like the Cosby's? Why can't you all just talk to me about stuff? Why are you always pressuring me and yelling at me and stuff? **SARAII**

When you tell somebody "don't", don't you know that's going to make somebody want to do it more? **JANAE**

SARAI

There's a lot of things going on. I have to worry about my mother sometimes because she's mentally ill. And I got to watch out for her, protect her and stuff, like in case something goes wrong. And my brother is caught up in the world – he likes to do all the gang signs and stuff. I be like, "Don't do that" but he don't listen to me.

I try to do a lot of things, but living in my house, you can't really do a lot of things. You can't depend on my mother and father. I want to go to driving classes and they won't come through. So I try to do a lot of things on my own because they don't really ever come through when I ask them for something.

They think because I'm sixteen I'm supposed to do stuff on my own just because when they got that age they were on their own. My father - he really strict - because when he got to that age he had to live on his own and stuff. When he was 14 he had a child– he lived in North Carolina, and then he left her and came to Baltimore and had me and my brother and stayed with my mother.

I try to follow my sister's influence. I just found out about this sister –and she went to college and everything. She married and she got two kids. She's a police sheriff for Winston-Salem. She's a sheriff, so I try to follow her influences too, because she doing something with her life. My father keeps saying get a job, get a job. And I tried to get a job but no one won't hire me. I tried Walgreen's, 7-11, Taco Bell, Wendy's, McDonalds. I went online and I filled out applications like a month ago and nobody came through, so I think it's like nothing will never come through for me. So, sometimes I feel sad. I always try to do stuff and nothing comes through.

My mother and father, they clothe me and give me all the

things I need, but they don't talk to me and that's why sometimes I just say that I don't like them. "I hate you, I hate you all." But I really love them. But they don't talk to me about the future and stuff. My parents don't never talk to me about nothing. They just tell me to go to my room, get off their phone, get off that game. My aunt talk to me, but not a long conversation. I really don't get a long conversation from anybody in my family – except my cousin. She give me a long conversation about my future, but she don't give me the present things. Like if I had something happen to me at school or something. I could tell them but I don't think they would do anything about it.

All they say is you better not do this, you better not do that, and sometimes I'm like why can't we be like the Cosby's or something? Why can't we live like the Cosby's? Why can't you all just talk to me about stuff? Why are you always pressuring me and yelling at me and stuff? That's what I just think. If they be more kind and nice and talk to me about stuff then maybe I would have a better understanding. When I tell them you all need to talk to me about stuff, they are like "You don't need no talking. You're almost grown. Get out of here."

LAKEDA

My mother works two jobs. She was a single parent until two years ago. She is going back to school to get her GED. Even though she has kids, she's still able to take care of me and both my brothers and manage to take care of the house and go to school so she can become a better parent and bring home more money so we can be financially stable.

I really look up to my mother because growing up she basically raised herself. She couldn't look forward to her mother doing anything for her. She dropped out of school when she was in the seventh or eighth grade so it was really hard for her. She had me when she was twenty-two. She's been a nurse for almost twenty years. I'm actually even proud of her because she's getting married on July 12.

I love my family. We are happy now, a happy family. My mother has accomplished a lot, and just to see her accomplish a lot, it builds my self-esteem. It helps me accomplish a lot.

DEINERA

The birth of my youngest brother is the most significant thing that has happened to me. Because of the way I act, he sees what I did and he do it. And I think that's motivation for me to change because I don't want my brother growing up doing the same things I done. So, I would say his birth was significant because it made me want to change a whole lot.

I can't speak about what makes a good parent, because with my mother being a single parent, and my father never really being there, I can only speak for my mother. I can't speak for no dads. A good mother is a woman that's strong and that got morals, goals and values. Somebody that never gives up even if you're going through something. If you fall down, you bounce back and get it together.

My mother taught me that life ain't easy. You got to work for whatever you want. Nothing comes easy. In order to be successful, you got to work. In order to be anything, you got to work. The struggles, how to survive - she definitely taught me how to survive because it's a crazy world.

ASHLEY

Listening to Ashley. *Ashley's quiet face sits off to the side of the room. Her dimples reveal youth and innocence. She doesn't interact with the class, but she loves to be called on. She loves to share her ideas. She is full of them, opinions and creativity. She is idealistic and has grown to love herself, her true self. The Ashley that we see is not the Ashley we get. Her shy demeanor can trick you into believing she is insecure, nonchalant and lacks an understanding of the world. However, she is confident, complex and sweet. She is brilliant but must be pushed--insightful but introverted.*

Taking the time to talk to her will reveal all of this and the fact that she is a watcher. She watches, dissects, analyzes, synthesizes and then creates. I didn't know she was watching me until I read the poem she wrote for me. She watched Eppy, a football player, and wrote about him too. We had some challenges with the school police and she wrote a poem that became the students' voice. I'm sure she was never a victim of the school police but she watched, she heard her classmates' complaints, and felt their pain and she wrote. I watched her too and wondered what was spinning in her mind.

[My mother] always talks to me. She always says "I love you." And, you know, that makes me feel special. It really does. I find myself speaking my mind, but my mother tells me it's just good to listen. I understand her. I totally understand her. But she gives me a look as though I don't understand her. I love her so much. She's always been there for me, hasn't been a time where I feel as though she has left me hanging. She's always been there for me.

And I feel as though when she does certain things, she wants me to learn responsibility. That's probably what it is. I just wish I could talk to her about it. I think she feels as though

I'm a teenager so that's what I'm automatically going to say. That's a defense mechanism for me. Like for me, a defense mechanism is saying that she is not – that she's not listening.

I think that she believes that most teenagers are going to think their parents are not listening, but all she's trying to do is just teach me responsibility and more independence. She wants me to be more independent, because I do find myself depending on her, but then I think to myself, I really cannot depend on her. I can't depend on her because she doesn't want me to depend on her.

The true Ashley is a lot of energy, a lot of high energy. I speak my mind, but not in a negative way, always in a positive way.

This is really my inner feelings and what I haven't told nobody. I do tell Cameron, though, and all my other friends like David and Destiny and they always help me out.

I feel as though I can be myself [at school]. And it's a shame you can be comfortable with people that are not related to you, but not your own family. I can be comfortable with anybody else in my house, especially when it comes to my step-father because he's really like my real father. Seriously, I see him as my real father. My mother thinks I give my biological father more praise than I do my step-father. That's not true. She doesn't understand what I am thinking in my head. She's not listening. My real father won't see how much anger I have built inside of me. As if I am going around saying, "I love David, that's my number one dad."

If you ever hear me talk about my dad, you'll hear me saying "Jamar." You'll hear me saying that because he's my hero. He's my number one dad. He's always been there for me. I can talk to him about anything. I can talk to him more than I can talk to my own mother. And I'm not mad at that. That's not something to be mad at. Because you're not always going to be able to talk to somebody. So that's a good, positive thing. He's my stepfather. He's somebody who's been put in my life.

So I feel as though that's good to get used to somebody where there's a really good connection to actually talk to him. And that's what she wants him to do, too. To just get used to my father and I'm really used to him now. He is my father and she thinks that I go around, "Oh, David is so a perfect father." If she only knew how much hate I have inside.

Usually I get mad when people don't talk to me because I just be thinking a whole bunch of thoughts that I have built up in my head. You cannot stop no matter how much stuff you say to somebody, trying to get them to talk to you. You're still going to have those thoughts in their head, you know, of thinking that "I hate her. I'm not going to talk to her."

When I am having a miserable time, I just can't take it. I just go upstairs in my room and I write poetry. Poetry is like my hero to me because it's always there for me. Nobody can ever touch my poetry. Not so much physically as they can pick up the book and read it, but as though they can never touch it, never say anything about my poetry that will ever hurt me in any way.

That's how I go back to the connection with my grandmother. She died. She had breast cancer. She wrote poetry, too, and I feel as though I connect with her. I didn't know she wrote poetry. My Uncle Michael actually told me [after she died]. He said she would say it off the top of her head or she would write it down. But, you know, I feel as though nobody can ever touch it. She's the only one who has that key to that lock. Me and her are the only ones who have that key. Nobody will ever get close to it. Nobody can ever bother me no matter how many times you rip up the poetry or throw it or you tear or spit on it, you'll never be able to touch it because it's always inside of me.

I just call [this poem] "Life."

I had a life and then you took it back.
You took everything from my future and relived it in my past.
I guess I should have never depended on you.
You are so special to me, but I was the opposite to you.
You did one thing right, I did another wrong.
I let you rob me of my beauty, dimples and all-
And when I try to look in a mirror, all I see is myself.
Not wanting a part of you made me appreciate me -
Me, just me and not you wrapped in it.
I want my life back and I'm not quiting.

DEAIRRA

A person that I look up to would be my mom because I watched her - I can't say necessarily "grow" because she's older than me of course - but she just overcame so many obstacles that it makes me look up to her. Because when I was younger she always made a way, no matter what, and never failed. If we needed something or if I needed something, I had it. And she never did nothing illegal. She just struggled to bust her butt to do it. Of course, I was a little jealous of my brother a little bit because hard times only came when I was born. My brother, he had it good. They had amazing Christmases. I see pictures and I think dag, my Christmas is never like that. I think I'm the only one out of my brothers and sisters that never had a real Christmas until 2004 when my grandma passed away.

My mother, she's just a strong being. She overcame two surgeries for her heart and a heart attack. She is the best. I just learned not to take things for granted. I'm not saying I didn't love my mother or care about her before, but it just made her more close to me, like she's my best friend and I tell her about everything. It's hard for a teenage child, being fifteen, but I tell my mother everything and I think she knows me like a book that she read fifty times.

I have, in a sense, two fathers because I have a sperm donor and then I have a father. Both of them are fathers because they do play their parts. When my mother was going through a hard time in her life, she met a man who made her happy because my father was cheating on her – well, the man we thought was my father, was cheating on her – and it was terrible and so when she found out she was pregnant, she thought it was the man she was in a long-term relationship with.

But when she had her first heart attack, she said she saw the man's face who she had relationship with in between her break-ups with my father and she just got in contact with him and came to find out that was my father. So once he found out he was my father, he played the part. He only had one son which was my brother Eric and at first he was a little shy. Of course, he'd be shy to find out you had an eight-year-old daughter. And then he just played his part, so I have two fathers who do well with me. I mean, they're not in my life all the time, but when they are in my life, we have a good time and they treat me right. So yeah, I have two fathers.

I wouldn't necessarily call it a benefit [to have two fathers] because it definitely has its hard times when one don't like the other. "Why is she doing that?" "Why is he doing that for her?" But, no, it's just a good thing I have more people to show my love to. I like putting a smile on people's face. I can honestly say that I put smiles on both of their faces.

Oh yes! I get treated different cause I'm a girl. Oh most definitely. But I'm going to say it's because my brother, he let the neighborhood pull him in, but he's doing well now. We live in Pigtown, in southwest Baltimore. Me and my brother have a gap because we're eight years apart. So we didn't necessarily grow up together, but that was my brother - you know what I'm saying? So growing up and seeing my brother, he got to go outside and come in the house like 10:30. I don't even have a curfew because I don't even come outside. My mother don't let me out the door. And so I would definitely say my brother had a lot more freedom.

I'm not going to say my brother's the reason my mother had a heart attack, but my brother was a stressful person. He was an intelligent person, but for him to throw it away by letting the neighborhood pull him in, my mother just didn't want me to get caught up in that. So now it seems like everything I do, I do it for my mother because I know that's what she wants me to do. I'm not saying that she's the reason why I'm doing everything, because I'm doing it for myself mainly, but just as like when my mother sees my report card and says "Oh look at that, you got Bs." She's my inspiration. I can say that.

AARON S.

Listening to Aaron S. *Aaron S. has a loud mouth that many times has no restraints. He took English two years in a row with his little sister. In class, they would argue as if they were home. She consistently wanted him to shut up and he consistently wanted her to mind her business. It was the typical sibling rivalry. However, you had better not say anything negative about either of them within earshot of the other. If you thought they hated each other you would soon find out* *they didn't.*

Aaron and I had a special routine. Aaron would walk in the room on time and then leave out or he would attempt to not show up at all. Sometimes I didn't notice but when I did, I broke the ultimate teacher code. I left my class to go and find Aaron. He wasn't ever very far; only a few rooms down or just in the hall. The class would work on their warm-up until I returned with Aaron in tow. It never failed they always seemed to think this was hilarious. More of them thought I was crazy for chasing Aaron down the hall.

From the time he walked in Aaron would not stop talking. If it was quiet he would blurt, "Man, it's too quiet in here! I can't take it!" These interruptions were fine with me because they are a lot less disruptive than the expletives that came out of his mouth. "Man, these niggas is some bitches Ms. Stone. My bad Ms. Stone, I'm sayin. Man you know what I'm sayin'." I knew what he was saying but I didn't want him to use profanity. Aaron is a prime example of students being different in school and outside of school. When I went to interview Aaron for this project, he was respectful, kind and he did not use profanity. I wasn't shocked because I knew that most students behave differently in school than they do outside of school.

A good parent is somebody who tells you every single day, get up. Get up. Go to school. That's one thing my mother do every day. And I ain't in the house. I can't be in the house unless I go to school. That motivates me, though. My mother make sure I get my diploma because she got hers. I got to go do high school. It has been like that since day one, since I can remember. Like since I've been in school. Got to go to school. She don't even want me to miss days. That's a good parent to me. School is first basically. Number one priority. School.

A man is somebody who take care of his own. Somebody who doesn't worry about anyone else but his self and his family and when he has to take care of his principles. Like my father. My father made sure – he put one of his kids through high school already. He want to put all of us through high school. He want to make sure all of us try to get through college, like he just making sure we do what we got to do. He make sure his kids got more than what he had when he was younger, or better things, anything. Just making sure you just do what you got to do.

I lost three home boys in 2008 due to gunshots, not nothing else, not no car accidents, not no strokes - gunshots. You feel me? Just by being a young black male. And it's not even white people killing us. It's us killing each other, so whereas people just get straight, you get dropped out here and worse. It's worse times three out here. Got to be on your p's and q's, everything. Just by having a father figure in your life, it just change your whole concept. Just by having somebody being on your back. "Boy, go to sleep. You got school tomorrow." Or "Boy, go wash your clothes for school tomorrow." " Go to work so you can go to school tomorrow." All right, yes. Just by having somebody on your back. A father figure. That changes your whole concept.

MADISEN AND JANAE

Madisen: I dislike parents who get mad at their daughters when they find out they're pregnant at a young age when they allowed them to stay out all hours of the night. They don't talk – they don't give them the parent-to-child talk, and they let them stay out all night.

Janae: Like my mother, she never sat down and talked

with me about sex or about boys or about my period or anything. I had to talk to friends and that's one thing that you should never have to do is talk to your friends because they don't know any more than you do. I had to talk to friends and my grandmother about it and like now my mother is letting me stay the night over my boyfriend's house. If I call her and say "Can you come pick me up?" she's like, "Well, I don't feel like it. Just stay the night." That's fine, but then the other day I asked her "What would you do if I was pregnant?" And she was like, "I would beat the daylights out of you." And I was like why? It's already done. Why would you do that? First of all, you're going to jail. Second of all, you allowed me to do it in the beginning so why try to do something now?

At some points, I enjoy the freedom because I do like doing what I want – but that's just me. I like to do what I want. But then, at another point it's like you're my mother. You're not supposed to be my friend. You're not supposed to allow me to do this. If I'm doing this, it's because I'm disrespecting you and you know you should still do something to punish me or something. It bugs me that she's like that, that she shouldn't have allowed me to do it.

I know when I was younger I used to make it seem like my mother is a good parent. My mother used to beat me. I used to go outside and say "I got a beating today." It was a good thing for me to go out and say that because it was like she's a real mother.

You know how we say how teenage girls depend on men or need a man in their life to help them get through? I feel like that's how my mother is and by me seeing that, it makes me want to be a better person and not be that way. So, in that way she did have a big influence on my life, but as far as anything positive that she do, I don't see anything positive and I don't want to be like her at all.

Madison: I did feel like that but I don't because my mother, she was a crackhead and I was the only one taking care of my two little brothers. That makes me want to be so opposite of her, like I really still despise her to this day, but she got herself together and so one side of me is saying you still did this, you still made me go through this and then one side of me is like you need to forgive, you need to forget. But I would like to be like her because she turned her life around and how she just tried her best to give me and my brothers the life that we didn't have.

Janae: My mother turned her life around. She always told me that she was never getting high, but just from growing up in the ghetto, you can just tell a crackhead. Even if you clean, keep yourself up and everything, you can just tell a crackhead. And she always says she didn't get high and I knew she was. She stopped - that's showing me that even when you're down and out that you can still get better. But at the same time, at the same point, like it don't matter if you change your life around or not – I still don't want to be like my mother. It's just from the things that she did, I just still don't want to be like her.

The only thing that my father's passed toward me as far as relationships is to never trust a boy. And sometimes I let my guard down and wind up do trusting them, but for the most part I do what he taught and play 'em. Get their money, get whatever they got, get from the men. It's not a good thing though, because you might run into somebody that is dangerous, like "You played me, you about to die." I have run into a boy like that. He wanted to kill me but I wouldn't let him get close enough. So for the most part it's dangerous but that's what I was taught.

Madisen: My father, he don't play, I mean, that's my father. My mother get mad because I have more of a relationship with my father than my mother. My mother do more for me now and my father did more for me when my mother was on drugs. So it's like all right – I love my father. I'm a daddy's girl.

Janae: I love my father more than I love my mother. You should never love one parent more than you love the other. They should both be equal. But I love my father more. My father was never there for me. I've been with my mother all my life. But whenever I called my father when I seriously needed him, he was there right away. When I needed my mother, and I've been with her all my life, she was never there. So, I happen to love my father more than I love my mother.

Madisen: My father, he's just a liar – liar, liar, pants on fire. He always say "I'm coming, all right." I'm going to get you this, I'm going to get you that. But it never gets done. But yes, I still love him like he's a god. I still worship him like he's God. And it's sad because my mother don't lie to me and anything I need she gives it to me and it's like I disrespect my mother because of what she did in the past.

Janae: I don't like my mother because just for the simple thing that she feels like she needs a man in her life and she don't.

Madisen: And she quit her kids. That's one thing you should never do. Never. A good parent is somebody that from jumpstart, when your child first starts going through puberty, sits their child down and talks about drugs.

Janae: Not even when they first start puberty. Before they even come about. My grandmother started talking to me I think I was seven. I didn't hit puberty until was 14, 15 – my grandmother was telling me what a cherry and everything else was. I had no idea what that stuff was – it's a piece of skin that gets popped when you have sex for the first time. I don't know whatever that thing is. That's called the cherry. And I didn't know nothing about it and she sat me down and was talking to me.

Madisen: Ain't nobody talking to me. My sisters just told me when you're ready to have sex, tell me and you're going to get put on birth control. But I was already having sex and then I told my mother– I want to have sex, right – I already had sex, and she was like all right. And my sister got mad at me , "Why ain't you tell me?" No, my mother like, my mother was hurt. I could tell she was hurt from the way she sounded.

Janae: Why should you be hurt if you don't want to sit down and talk to me and tell me why I shouldn't? All you want to tell me is don't. What is don't? When you tell somebody don't, don't you know that's going to make somebody want to do it more?

What Could Happen Four Days Before Christmas?

By Yvonne

Who would have thought this would happen? On the day of December 21, 2006, I saw my father get locked up.

It all started when my mother and father woke up for work. My father always took my mother to work and then he came back home. This time, he came home too soon. The police had been plotting on my house for some days now, but no one knew anything about it. That morning as soon as my father came back in the house the police came banging.

Everybody in the house awoke. My father started to panic. He told my older brother and sister to hide him. He went in his room and got in the closet and told them to put a lot of clothes on top of him. He didn't expect his younger kids to do anything because we didn't know what was going on. So they began to do what my father said.

The police kept banging saying "Open up" but no one answered. My two young sisters were so scared, so they went in their room and closed the door. The police counted down, "One, two, three," then began to bang the door down. Once they got into my house they began to search. The police then became disrespectful to my two young sisters. The police pointed a gun into my two sisters' room and they were very scared. All I heard was screaming and crying. Then they headed to my room and I began to cry. The next thing I knew they went in my mother's and father's room and began to look around for him. My mother didn't know what was going on at home because she was at work.

I hear a big bang and we think my father is hurt. They

find him. I start to cry even harder. They put him in hand cuffs and take him outside. My big brother gets very angry and starts banging holes in the walls. The police say "Stop son, before you be going where you father is going." I say "Who is going to fix our door?" The police try to be smart and say "Your father when he gets out of jail." My sister starts to get smart with the police. The sheriff says, "Who else lives here with you all?" and we responded "Our mother." The police tell us to call her or they would take all of us to a foster home. We call our mother and tell her what happened and she says she is coming home. The police then ask to speak to my mother and tell her that our father was hiding behind his kids. The police wait until my mother comes and then leave.

I knew were were not going to get nothing for Christmas because my father's bail was $1500.00. I was mad at my father. When he would call I would not talk to him. My mother and father said they would get the stuff we wanted after Christmas. They said they would make it up to us because my mother could not do it on her own.

Then I realized that I wanted my father out of jail more than I wanted gifts for Christmas. So my father got home Christmas morning. I had a gift after all! I was so happy to see him. The biggest thing I learned out of all that is my father is more important than Christmas.

2

TEACHERS AND SCHOOL

The worst thing that a teacher could do is give up on the students. **DEINERA**

The government should get rid of the No Child Left Behind program. The program doesn't leave <u>a</u> child behind because it keeps <u>all</u> the children behind. **HEATH**

School is for when you go there you got a second mother or second father. So if society is not providing good teachers, whoever pay the teachers - they not on their job basically. Because when I go to school, I look for having a second mother, a second father, somebody to put me in my place and tell me what I got to do. **AARON S.**

AARON S.

The best piece of advice anyone has every given me is to stay in school. Everyday I'm outside I look at junkies and crackheads and dopeheads and half of them ain't stayed in school and I'm pretty sure that's most of the reason they the way they is. I want to say God keeps me off drugs but I would say that not being in school provokes them to go ahead with the drugs because they ain't got nothing else to do. They can't go get a job. They can't go to the market and put food in the house because they ain't got no job or no money. So, they just go on with drugs, I guess.

A good teacher is someone who listens, somebody who wants to hear what you're going through every day. They ain't just coming to school and coming to get that check. Basically a second mother or father—a school mother or father - tells you right from wrong and makes sure you ain't doing wrong.

My first two years at Southside I had good teachers, real good teachers. The ones that just listened to me, made sure I'm going to do what I got to do to get out of here. I'm going to leave with my diploma basically. Second mothers and fathers.

But there ain't too many teachers in Baltimore City that come to school and really want to put up with kids all day long. They come to school and they give you work and you go home. We got a lot of vacancies in teachers. There's not even many good teachers - no, more like it's rarely some. And if it is some, they the ones that have been in the system for about fifteen years or twenty years. They're used to it and ready for us. But like when we get a lot of new teachers straight out of college - kids are looking at them as if they're kids because they're young - so they act like they outside, like they is they peers at the end of the day. So, I think it should be probably a lot more older teachers, but like all people don't come from the same place. So there are some teachers that come from Baltimore City and have already been through the school system, just like us. I ain't going to say everyone like that, but it's a lot of teachers like that now. I guess that's being a good teacher. Listening.

I went to West Baltimore Middle School where we basically did what we want. I can really say that. I came to school, we came to school and we passed. Just because we made it. If you got marked on attendance, you passed. That's what I can really say. But when I come in Southside, I come in there to work. I got to pick up that pen and pencil and come in there with that notebook, that uniform on ready to work. It's like a job. And if you don't work, you'll get fired just like a job.

The schools need money. Give us money, man. They been getting us [in high school] for a couple years now. I remember when I was growing up and I was going to elementary school and –I used to like going to school. Now school make me don't even want to go now. We ain't got what we used to have. I can say that back then I was in elementary school we had summer school. We got to pay for summer school now. In Baltimore City, it's $150 a class. That stops a lot of people from even getting diplomas, getting credits, everything. A lot of people don't even got $150 to go get a pair of shoes or go do nothing. People ain't got money to pay for summer school, so that right there just kill a lot of people in high school. You know in high school now you got to have seventy-five community hours, service hours. And all your HSAs, you got to pass all your HSAs tests, it's like four of them. And you got to have your credits, twenty-one credits just to even get a diploma. It's crazy like – so many people can't even complete that. People don't know how to do community service. I can name ten of my home boys that don't even know how they're going to do community service hours. Don't know how to walk to a church and say can I cut your grass so you can give me some community service hours. I know 10 people don't know how to do that. It's just crazy.

Because just like I said, school is number one. Your parents are supposed to teach you from jump. But, if they lack on it or if they don't show you, like I said, school is for when you go there you got a second mother or second father. So if society is not providing good teachers, I would say the government or anybody, whoever pay the teachers - they not on their job basically. Because when I go to school, I look for having a second mother, a second father, somebody to put me in my place and tell me what I got to do.

TARENA

School's not worthwhile all the time because sometimes you got some teachers that just come to get paid. And I don't like when teachers try to put kids down, like "You're not going to make it in life if you keep doing all this." They're not supposed to do that. You're supposed to build their confidence up. Even if they're not doing good, still tell them to keep their head up: "You can do better." You've got some teachers who say "Oh, you keep acting that way you're going to be working at McDonald's." Ain't nothing wrong with that. Some kids, like us, 14 and 15, we want a job, that's the only job we can get. That's the only job that they're hiring. I can be making straight A's in school and I want a job and if McDonald's the only job and they're hiring, that's where I'm going to work to get some money. Like, "Oh, she ain't go to school or she ain't got a diploma, look where she's working at." That don't mean nothing. I could have my diploma, college degree and still work at McDonald's.

A good teacher explains stuff to you when you need help. Not just give you something, not just tell you, because you've got some kids that don't understand stuff on the first go-around. When teachers give us work, don't just give it to us and just put it in our face. At least explain to us what you want us to do. Make it fun. 'Cause kids are going to want to do work if it's fun, once it's explained. Also, a good teacher is a teacher that not just helps you with your school work, they can help you with your problems and everything. And, like, if you're going through something at home, they can help you out with stuff. They can be your friend, but on a certain level. Like some teachers don't talk to kids because they ignorant, don't know what to say out of their mouths.

MALCOLM

We've got something like two teachers that be teaching us. You got teachers who just come and sit down like Ms. C--. She just sits there and stay on the computer and digs in that little refrigerator and pulls snacks out all day and eats. And the students are sitting there failing. And then when we take our exams, she wonders why we fail. A teacher should be like your parents. They should care about you. They should ask you what's going on in your life and all that, unless the kid is ignorant.

DELORIS

Patience is a virtue. I don't have it, and that's why I be in class zapping and stuff because it's boring me. Like pick it up! Sometimes in class you have the really slow people that want to keep asking questions about the same thing you just went over for the past twenty minutes. Look, if you don't got it, move on teacher! If you don't got it, you just don't have it. It's not for you. That's why most of the time I get in trouble in class. And then, if something is boring me, I just move on to the next thing. The teacher be like "You remember such and such?" And I just be talking.

CHOC

Education is the key nowadays, you know. You can't do nothing without an education, I feel as though like I need my high school diploma, so that's really important – education. I go to a Harlem Park school now, because I got put out Southside. Got caught in the bathroom with some marijuana or whatever. When I got put out, I was real stuck for real. Southside a good school. So I was real mad for a while - I was angry that I got put out.

I was angry at myself, angry that the principal put me out – the whole thing – me bringing weed to school and stuff like that. I wasn't thinking ahead of myself. I wasn't thinking. I just had it on me, I wasn't smoking it.

At Southside, the teachers, they believe in you or whatever. And I feel as though at Southwestern [High School] they're just there to, I don't know what to say about it. There's just a better teaching environment at Southside. I'm not really learning nothing at Harlem Park for real. The teachers were better, a better environment at Southside, I think. Southside teachers, they gave a lot of advice, stuff like that. Like when I got shot, the teachers at Southside, they came and see me in the hospital. They was real supportive. They was real supportive and at Harlem Park, they like, I mean, if you don't come to school –

you don't come to school, I mean, they don't try to push you to come – if you don't want to be there, they say don't come. At Southside they force you to come to school. They were forcing, asking when you ain't come to school, "Where were you at?" "Everything okay?" And at Harlem Park, it's like, oh man, it's just not the same.

A good teacher has to be there teaching. You got to teach me. Youth, we like somebody to motivate us for real, so a teacher should be a motivated person. Just show them that you care for real, just showing that you care about us. That's how we want things. I just feel as though like teenagers need support in whatever they do. Just give us a little push or a little advice here and there to keep us on the right path for real. Have faith in our youth, you know. We're the future. So I feel as though like yeah, that is the worst thing you can do is give up on us. That's the last thing we're looking for you to do, no matter how much we mess up, we'd still like you to have faith in us and tell us what we're doing wrong or what we're doing right or what we can to better ourselves.

JANAE

Listening to Janae. *Janae is passionate. She seems reserved but she is outspoken and wholeheartedly feels and believes what she says and thinks. In the ninth grade, Janae was a scholar. She was in school everyday, although she was late. She was a diligent student; she completed all assignments and contributed intensely to all class discussions. In the tenth grade something changed. Her emotions would be up one day and down the next. The obstacles she faced at home affected her schoolwork, her attitude about school and her overall attitude. "I don't know what's wrong with me.*

I just don't care no more." I didn't have an answer either. I gave her a journal. I figured that getting out whatever it was that was nothing could help. It seemed to intensify. As a senior, she has seemed to settle into who she is and maintains her diligent efforts to graduate.

    I actually feel like all my teachers care about us learning – every teacher that I have, I think they care about us learning or care about me learning. So it can't be the teachers. I think it's because of all the family problems that I had and trying to have a relationship [with a boy] because a relationship is very stressful, especially when you're going to school. And just having a whole bunch of problems. When you get to school you can't focus so I guess that's what made me not like it. Now, I'm starting to focus a little bit more and I think it's just because I want to graduate. Just because I want to get out of school so I don't have to worry about coming and focusing. The only thing that could mean more to me, I just want to have my own house and I think that's another problem. Just trying to be grown is stressful and it doesn't allow you to do what I need in school.

    A good teacher would come to school every day and make sure that you're here on time and if you're not they would ask you questions about why you're not here and is it something they can do to help you get here on time. Or if you're not focusing, that they are "What's wrong with you?" Just talking so you can get whatever it is off your chest or maybe you can focus better. Trying to talk to you like, being the parent while you're away from your parents.

    As far as school goes, I know that I need an education to be what I want to be, but I really could care less about coming to school or going to college or whatever. But I know that I need it. When I was in the ninth and tenth grade I actually loved coming to school. I would get up early in the morning like "I'm ready to go to school." But now it's like I just don't like it and I don't know what happened. Like I really don't know what happened.

TORI

Listening to Tori. *I met **Tori** during the Summer Bridge program we sponsored for the incoming 9th graders. She sat in the cafeteria writing a story. "You're a writer?" I asked.*

"Well, no not really, but I'm writing a story."

I squinted my eyes. "You're writing a story?" Tori shook her head.

"Well you're a writer."

"But I just write them and keep them in my notebook. I just write them for fun. I mean I like it."

"You're still a writer."

This is her second year at Southside and my prayers were answered. I get to have Tori in my class. Today she is a mime and she refuses to speak. She has on white gloves, a black skirt, black and white stockings and a black shirt. "What are you today, Tori?" Akea laughed. Tori kind of made a face and shrugged her shoulders. "I think she's a mime," I suggested.

"So you ain't gon' say nothing?" Akea asked, still laughing relentlessly.

Yesterday Tori was a geisha, complete with a kimono-like dress and bright red rouge and lipstick to match. A few days ago she was a boy. She is an individual- so much so she baffles her classmates. However, it seems the humor they find in her daily transformations only fuel her desire to be different. Tori, a.k.a Discovery Channel, strives to do her best in class. She has a strong desire to excel. Among a group that has a strong disdain for excellence, she soars. When the class is off she is still on. There were days when Tori and I had class alone and others were simply spectators. Many days I looked forward to third period because she was there and I knew someone wanted to learn. While others complained about the work being boring or dumb, Tori worked. She listened, asked questions and made connections. Tori--the epitome of a scholar.

Southside isn't rich. I would say it's probably a poor school, but it's not a bad school. It's not some school where you'd be in danger going there. Children think they're dangerous, but they're not, you know. I never encountered any problems. Maybe somebody saying something to me, but it's a safe school. It's kind of poor but we have our stuff that we enjoy here still. And I get enough education from here so I guess it's okay, because the teachers are good.

The students here – they don't want to learn because it's boring to them. I personally think it's boring anyway. But in Ms. E---'s class, their behavior does disrupt the class a lot because they try to walk all over her and stuff. Except for being quiet and sleeping and bored, they're loud, you know, talking over her and stuff. And it really gets in the way of my learning, like really bad. Can't hear stuff, you know. Can't write down my notes. It's stopped a little bit. I'm angry that they don't care about anyone else in the room. They think that everyone wants to play around and everyone's bored with the lesson and no one wants to learn it. And I really love chemistry and they just talking and stuff, you know, nobody wants to learn this. I do. There is like three people in the class that wants to learn. It's sad.

Some classmates call me "history channel" or "discovery

channel." I was talking about this with my mother. It flatters me, but then again it kind of gets on my nerves. They make me seem smarter than I am - because they're smart too. They just don't try. You know, they look at the work and say, "Oh, this is too hard." It's one BCR [brief constructed response] – "it's too hard." They don't try. I feel as though they're kind of jealous because they think that I'm bragging, "Yeah, I'm smarter than you." Their confidence and self-esteem is low, so they think that. But I'm not. It doesn't really bother me, though, it's a compliment, actually.

DEINERA

Listening to Deinera. *Deinera is outspoken. If she sees something wrong you better believe she is going to acknowledge it, let someone know that it should be fixed and how to fix it. "Ms. Stone, you need to quit. You just don't care anymore. You are not Ms. Stone, you're Anna. You are not the same teacher I had. You just gon' let them sit there and not do their work?"*

She made an accurate observation. She was actually trespassing. She had been expelled from Southside for a fight she had with a few students on the city bus. "See y'all lucky cause she wasn't havin' that when I was in her class." She looked around the room and shook her head. She had been out of my class for two years and she was right. I had been worn down. More often than not she was right but because as adults we want children to "stay in their place" we don't acknowledge their insight, expertise or knowledge. After all, we are the adults and we are supposed to know. This type of outspokenness is what kept Deinera in trouble.

"No Ms. J-- not gon' talk to me like that! I don't care

who she think she is. She gon' write me up cause I said I hope her plane crash – 'cuz I do. She gon' tell the class she the reason our mothers get welfare. I hate her! She don't know my mother. She think she better than us. Then the other day during the fire drill she gon' say no you stay in the buildin'. She ain't right. That's why I said I hope her plane crash."

Her mother is strict, but Deinera is stubborn. There are rules and expectations, but to Deinera fun and freedom are far more valuable than stern lectures or being punished. "I mean you only have one life Ms. Stone. I don't know about you but Imma enjoy mine." To some she would seem to lack restraint but restraint is only invoked when absolutely necessary—that means her life is in jeapordy.

"I'm not trying to get smacked by Ruby." Ruby is Deinera's mother. You must have Deinera's respect for her to listen. Neither your title nor your position of authority grants you respect. You must earn it. She is also a talented poet.

I had a teacher once that was really, really dedicated. I really, really enjoyed her class. I had been struggling with math like my whole life – but I had a teacher that made math easy to me, that made math fun to me, that made me actually want to be in her class and actually want to do math. I had a lot of teachers that were good at what they did and I enjoyed their classes.

A good teacher is dedicated - a teacher that wants to do it. Because if a teacher's attitude is that he or she doesn't want to do it, it's not going to motivate the children. As long as the teacher is dedicated, the teacher is able to teach. It's something that a teacher wants to do, therefore it can be done.

The generations of students are different. My generation, we wanted to do it. And our teachers made it fun. They made learning fun. The teachers are slacking. They get in there, they hand us work and they say "Do this." They explain it a little bit, but when I was in ninth and tenth grade, it just was fun. You looked forward to going to class because your teachers were so uppity and everything. But I will say there's nothing you can do. It's the generation. The kids are different. More money for education would change nothing. By me being a kid, I'm going to tell you honestly the generations have changed. And the kids just – they don't care no more. School's not important.

I really think it has a lot to do with the parents because the parents got to be determined. They got to be – like I said, my mother is headstrong. They got to let kids know how important school is and then maybe they will want to do it. The teachers got to boost their spirits. They got to make us think that this is what they want to do because if this is what they want to do then we're going to want to do it. But if the teacher don't want to do it, then we're not going to want to do it.

The worst thing that a teacher could do is give up on the students, go to the principal and say "I don't want these five in my class, get them out." That's the worst thing you could do. Like I said, you give up on them, they give up on theirselves. I would have to say be patient, because if the other twenty-five are doing the work – if this is what they want to do - they're going to continue to do it with the five disturbing them or not.

There's a reason why those five are acting the way they are. I'm not going to lie - elementary and middle school, I would act up in the class just so the teacher could lean on me. Get a couple laughs. If you give them the spotlight, that's what they want. When the teacher fuss at one student, the class gets quiet. And everybody just listens to them just argue back and forth. That's what the student wants. Honestly, I will honestly tell you that. So, you would just have to be patient. Try to ignore them. Don't pay them no mind and they eventually see

"I look stupid – I keep yelling out, keep throwing stuff, keep doing this, keep doing that, and ain't nobody pay me no mind."

I can't really put myself in a teacher's situation but with my personality, I would kick [the misbehaving students] out. I would say, "Hey, you've got to go." But I wouldn't advise a teacher to do that because they act that way in every other class. Every other teacher probably kick them out. If you're that one teacher who doesn't, they're going to really sit back and like, this teacher not giving up on me. This teacher is really making me do this, making me do that. They're going to want to do right. When they do little stuff right, award them. Not award them but you know, "Hey you did this today, I'm happy you did this." Because they like that positive attention. They like negative attention too. Any attention they strive for.

When I was going to Southside Academy, you are family. If I was being so smart, everybody stuck together. It wasn't too much fighting. We was a family. If somebody needed help, you got help. The teachers was dedicated, the majority was dedicated and really wanted to do what they were doing. At Lake Clifton [High School] the teachers - I won't say they didn't care, but if you didn't get it done, it wasn't their problem. It was like whatever. If you don't do it, that's your fault. You fail, not me. At Southside, the teachers, they really wanted you to do it and not saying they were so bad if you wouldn't have done it, but they would have been disappointed.

If a teacher pushes you and you see that somebody really cares, really wants you to do something, you might play like you don't care. But in the back of your head, you say dang, I know I let this person down or I let that person down. And it's going to get to you. It'll get to you.

By me going to Lake Clifton, I didn't know too many people there. By the teachers not really caring, I stopped caring. I stopped caring and just gave up. They gave up on me. I gave up on myself. I feel like at Southside I might have played around for a little while longer, but if them teachers would have continued to push me, I'd have got it done.

HEATH

I did horrible on my studies in middle school. I think 76 [percent] was my average. I didn't care. I was one of those kids that didn't care. I mean, I cared – I love knowledge and I taught myself a lot of what I know in science and stuff, because I have an interest in that and at a young age I just threw myself into it. But the teachers there did not care, so why would I care? They gave me that negative attitude towards learning. I mean, not towards learning, but towards being there. All the teachers I've had at Southside have been good. Like Ms. Stone - I've had Ms. Stone two years in a row. I've had Ms. G--. I've had Mr. Z--, who taught me a lot of humor and about life.

The problems in Baltimore City schools started by lowering the passing grade. When I went to [middle] school it was 70 [percent]; now it's 60 [percent], so more kids don't have to retake the class - it will get them out of the school faster. But it's also holding people back. In classes we go over lessons over and over and over again because the kids, they don't listen. They don't want to listen. They can just get a 60 and cruise right on through. That just takes away from me and my education because I have to sit there and listen to that lesson over and over again and we don't have time. We don't get to the next lesson and it just takes away from my time and my education.

I would like different language classes, other than Spanish. But I can understand why Spanish is required, it is the next language in the United States. It's popular. And other things like better computer classes than Business Tech which just taught us to do business stuff with computers and courses like that-- an art course.

I think they should keep the HSAs [high school assessments], but a lot of what we do in school is HSA practice, or it's benchmark practice. You're not interested in that course. You're just going to do this work to take that test and pass it. Instead, they could be teaching better things, things that would interest you more in that field other than test practice, test practice, test practice. In high school you have a set curriculum, but when you get into college you can pick your majors and minors and stuff, but how are you supposed to know what you're interested in when you're just doing all these practices for tests? High school has got the window, you can see the window, but it's locked. You can't get through it.

The kids don't think that they have to pass every HSA, they just have to get a composite grade to be able to graduate. I think that was stupid, too, because –you just hear students, it's like oh, "I'm not worried, I'll just get it, you know, I have to pass a few of these or I can pass this class. I can fail her exam and if I can get 50s in the class and pass her exam, I can pass." How are you going to do that if you've been failing her class? How are you going to pass the final exam if you're going to do that?

The government should get rid of the No Child Left Behind program. Because I think that the program doesn't leave *a* child behind because it keeps *all* the children behind. So how can anyone be left behind since all are left behind? I don't know if you'd be able to fix the problem, but it's kids – their morale is just not there. They don't have the will to learn. They don't want to learn. I don't know how that happened. I don't know. I just noticed that it happened. They don't want to be here, but they know they have to be here and since they don't want to be here, it's like they don't care what they're doing. "I don't care if you're giving me this paper. I'm not going to do this paper. I'm not going to listen to you. I'm just going to sit here and talk to my friend because she came." You know? And then, that sucks because you're giving up this really great chance to learn and get all this knowledge and you don't care.

Why?

I love knowledge. How could you not want it? I mean, it's not good or evil, you know, it's neutral and you can do whatever you want with it. You can do really great things with it. You can do stupid things with it. And why would you pass up the chance to have something like that? I think kids are just stupid. That's my theory. They're stupid. They don't have the will to do it. I think it's because they have such low expectations of themselves. You know – "I'm from Baltimore. I'm not going to amount to anything. Why even try?" And that's why, you know, they just don't care.

DARIOUS

Listening to Darious. *When **Darious** arrived in the ninth grade he was quiet but did not respect authority. He was angry and I wasn't sure why. He was a good student. He completed class assignments and participated when called on but if he didn't want to do something, it wasn't going to get done.*

One day, Darious bragged about having pounds of marijuana in his locker. I knew he was playing but he was disturbing my class with his antics. The school police officer walked by my door and I quickly called him into my room and made him aware of Darious' claims. He took him into the hall. I was hoping to instill a sense of fear. I wanted him to understand that you just don't say things like that. Officer

R-- searched him, forced him to open his locker and searched it as well.

Darious stood with a straight face and never flinched. There was no fear nor any reaction for that matter. Maybe it was because he knew he didn't have drugs in his locker. I never considered that this is something he endured daily in his own neighborhood. When I saw his reaction, I felt awful. I thought about why he couldn't possibly care less about being searched by the police.

We battled a couple of times after that but in tenth grade he loosened up, maybe because I wasn't his teacher. Maybe it was because of the outing he, Deinera and a student named Wilbeck and I took to Dave and Busters and the movies. He said he never had a teacher take him anywhere.

Schools need a good principal, teachers who will work with the children, and more concerned staff, who are concerned about children and like they got to work with them. They could be their teacher and like a friend at the same time but then you know your place at the end of the day. Some teachers just teach for the paycheck. "Oh, I don't care, you going to fail." You're supposed to work with the children. We have some kids that have a bad attitude, but you're going to have some bad kids. Give them that right talk, then you might change the whole perspective.

There was one teacher I had – Mr. B--. I was sitting in class and he was trying to put me out of the class and I was like ten minutes left in class. I told him it was no reason for me to leave, I mean, I was doing my work. He thought that I was being disruptive. So, we stood. It was face to face with a desk in between us and I moved to the side. He had a big ruler in his hand and he just pushed me out of his way, pushed me away so I fell. And when I got back up, I hit him one time and walked away. I could have done more, but I didn't. At the end of the day – I guess I was in the wrong – I had to go to court, proven guilty, put on probation. I tried to use self-defense and they said it wasn't no self-defense in Maryland.

Mr. B—, he ain't get no consequences. I think he should have got more consequences than me because he touched me first. If anything he was the teacher. But they said since I never really came to them [school administrators] and I assaulted him afterwards, I guess I was in the wrong. I should have just came to the principal. So, I regret doing it, but then I was just defending myself at the same time.

At Southside, there was a few teachers who cared about us. There was a few who didn't, they were just there just to get a paycheck. And then our principal – she don't know how to work with children. Her attitude against children or against the students - like she supposed to portray a different attitude. Like she mad all the time. At us, for no reason. And she don't know what we could be going through at home. And then when you come to school and her attitude reflects on us, that probably drive somebody crazy. Don't know what the students are going through now these days.

The school system can be much better. They could give us more money toward all Baltimore City schools. I know in certain schools like the top-notch schools - Poly and Mervo and City - they getting all this money and endorsements while other schools just read old textbooks from 1996 and ain't getting no money. We got to go out there and raise our own money - fundraisers.

The way that I think teachers make students do their schoolwork and take it more serious, they have to put it in a way that a student can understand much better. Every student is not that smart. So you saying all these big words and you have all this powerful vocabulary we're not going to understand. Most teachers don't even teach you. They just talk. They just go over the lesson. We not even learn nothing all day. And then give us a quiz about it, and think I'm supposed to know. Be more – like I was saying earlier, be more as like a friend. You could talk to me, you can be my teacher and talk to me like I'm one of your friends, but at the end of the day I know that I got parents. If I don't do my work, you're not going to help me out more. I'm going to have to do my work, but you're just going to have to be more concerned.

GAGE

Teachers have to be understanding of the student. They can't think that what *they* think is what the children should do because children have their own separate views. We need to express that individually.

Why are schools not performing well? Every school that I know, that I've been to, we've never performed well on tasks. Once every now and then we start performing well. The government should give more money to schools because I see graffiti all over the school walls and scratches on the doors and they could do something to make it more homey. Have people paint on the walls, put their own view and what they like on the walls. It will be more appealing to us, make us want to come here. Make us do stuff, give us more activities to do after school, fund more activities.

I wish someone would solve school security. We have cops and all, but they force the kids to move and they know they can't do that. They have to be persuasive and help them and enrich them and try to get them to move out of the hallway and stop throwing up gang signs and everything, clack, clack, clack clack, bam, bam, bam, bam.

TYESHA

This school food is nasty. They need to give us some fried chicken and stuff like that and put all that onions in our brains. I get food poisoning every other week from this food. I get a stomach virus. I'm too skinny to be throwing up all my food. I be trying to hold it down.

The teachers act like they don't care; *some* of them act like they don't care. A teacher who cares - like when we do our work and stuff like that, if we need help, they'll help us. Some of them, they just sit right there and do nothing. One of my teachers, I asked him for some help and to put it on the board, but he wouldn't put it on the board because I didn't understand. So if I fail this test, it's going to be his fault when it comes up. It do happen a lot.

It was national cut week last week and everybody knew about it. All high schools knew about it. The principal don't ever walk around the school on a regular basis, but she walks around the school when it's like fifteen people here, which it was like fifteen people [last week]. I came. I came to get my work and then I left. We went to Chuck-E-Cheese. That's where the meet-up spot was at.

MELISSA

I hate the principal. She gets on everybody's bad side. She put me on a conduct sheet just for leaving school early. Because I got tired of Mr. O--, I walked out of the class and I walked out of the school. I was on a do-not-admit list. I walked out a couple of days ago, I didn't get caught, though. I didn't get caught.

I'm passing all my classes. I got an 80, 60, 80, 90. And I'm cutting this week. I'm cutting tomorrow.

SARAI

I'm on the honor roll. I was happy. They sent me a letter and then they told me to fill out this thing and then they told me to send it back and then I did and they sent me another letter and they're supposed to post my name in a book, in an honor roll book and it's supposed to come back to Southside and they're going to announce it on the intercom. I was happy when I found out that I was on the honor roll.

I always try to do stuff and nothing comes through. Like, I failed that one exam- I failed Ms. Stone. Ms. Stone, I always pass her class. I always pass her class with like 95's and 100's and everything. And then I failed her exam. I was crying. I don't know how I failed her exam when that's the only class I actually can get through. And then I pass math and I'm looking like math ain't my favorite subject. Math? I suck at math. I can't do math. And I'm looking like, I passed math with an 80? I don't even know how to add and subtract, how can I pass math? And then I was just mad. But I wasn't that mad because I only failed one exam. But I was mad – But Ms. Stone said Ms. A-- graded them. I thought if Ms. Stone would have graded them that I would have gotten a higher grade.

I'm trying to get transferred out of this school We really don't learn anything. We learn stuff, but we don't get better understandings of everything and our teachers barely come and stuff. Some teachers, they just don't care about their students. I'm a student and I learn, I try to learn and do the work and stuff. I listen. I pay attention. And when other students try to distract the class, disrupt the class, the teacher stops and stops everybody from learning, so I can't get my education. So that's why I think they should just take the students who want to disrupt out of the class, don't give them no second chance because they're just going to keep doing it. And teach the ones that want to learn. But instead they just stop.

And sometimes I think that teachers don't really, really care. All teachers do is try to come to school and they just get paid for not doing anything. They just don't care. If you want to learn, you want to learn. If you don't want to learn, you won't want to learn. But if that's the case, why don't they just take the students that want to learn and take the students that don't want to learn and put them somewhere and take all the students that do want to learn and put them somewhere. My mother wanted me to get a transfer. So that's why I have to get transferred. But they said it's a three-hour test to get into Carver.

Today in Ms. Stone's class, the students asked her why she was so angry. And she said, say if I said I was hungry, and she put a plate of food in front of me - some steaks, mashed potatoes, some broccoli - and she said, "There you go, there's something to eat." And I still said I'm hungry, she'd be like, "The food's right there." I'm like, "I'm hungry," and she's like "Why don't you eat the food there?" That's how she feels about learning. We get free education and then we don't want to learn. But I take any education that I can get. I really do – I really want to learn.

DEAIRRA

From what I see at my school, the financial side is very low.

Like, I went to Poly the other day – their school was so laid out – they have a pool. They have everything. I'm in a JROTC program and they had an Air Force program, and their air force has a flight simulation room where you actually have a steering wheel and the pedals to teach you how to fly the airplane. And it's crazy, because like at Southside, we don't have that. We have the JROTC room and we just got weapons. We just received our weapons not too long ago. So I think the funds are very low and if we had a lot more money, we might be able to do some stuff.

We should have volunteers in the school, honestly. Some people out there who just love art. Why can't they come to the school and volunteer to teach an art class? You never know. Somebody might donate money out of their pocket to pay for that. It shouldn't be all about the money thing because if you love what you do, you should do it no matter what if you're getting paid or not. It's got to be something else they're doing. Art makes money too. But in the same sense if you love it so much, you should be able to volunteer and do it for students who love it. If students don't have nothing to do in school except but just four or five classes that are required to graduate, then some people stop coming to school because they feel as though they're not doing nothing that I want.

Our school is definitely, definitely on the academic level. Ain't no doubt in my mind because most of our kids go to college. It never fails. I don't see the papers, but when I talk to seniors that graduated last year, most of them are in college. So it's no different academically because all of us are smart. Well, we do have a few knuckleheads, but the majority of us are smart.

A good teacher is someone who basically has a good connection with the students. I don't care how boring the class is, if you've got a connection with that student, then she comes in, or he comes in that class. My teacher Ms. Stone – her class is dry, but I just love her so much. I come to her class and I just got to do it, especially when she call my mother. I don't like getting in trouble, but I like when a teacher cares so much that they actually sit there and tell your mother – but Ms. Stone, she did it in a good way. She told my mother what I was doing wrong, I didn't come to her class, but in the same sense she told my mother the good stuff I do too. I think there's not a lot of teachers who tell the parents, "Well, this person has done something bad, but they do something good too." They always tell the negative side more than the good side.

School is sexist to me because they expect girls to do better than boys in school and I know this really young man who don't come to school at all and passes all his tests. So I think school's a waste on him in that sense, but other than that, I don't know because last year a friend of mine went to the nurse's office – she was getting all her tests done and the nurse was like, "Oh well, I should expect that." So it was sort of like she was saying she knew why she was here, that she's fresh, and the nurse didn't know her from Adam and Eve. We were freshmen coming in, so that made me upset about that too because why do all girls have to be fresh? You don't even know them. They just judge a book before they read the book.

I'm going to narrow it down for African Americans because they feel as though African American males are - I'm not going to say worthless because I know they're not worthless - but that's how some people view it in so many ways if you look at it. It's like oh, all they want to be is drug dealers, gang bangers and deal on corners. But I have known a lot of African American males who do their work, are quiet as a mouse in class and of course when they do go outside they have their fun and roughhouse and play, but that doesn't change their effect or the opinion in school.

AARON C.

Since I've been at Southside I've been suspended probably three times. Three times I've been suspended, but I had a couple of parent/teacher conferences and I even got expelled from Southside twice. They put me out one time, sent me to Harbor City [High School] for 45-day suspension and then I was supposed to be at Harbor City earlier this year. But Southside accepted me back.

I got put out the first time because me and one of my home boys was inside the bathroom. Me and Choc was in the bathroom and Officer R-- came in there and Choc had marijuana all rolled up in a cigar and he flushed the toilet. I just knew he flushed it down the toilet before [Officer R—arrived]. But either way I knew I was in trouble because I came to school with a blade in my left pocket, something I shouldn't have did, but I found it when I walked to school and I just picked it up. I didn't think I was going to be in no trouble and I wasn't planning on getting caught on school property with the knife. I was planning on coming around here and using it for some protection. But I got caught. I got expelled.

The second time they put me out because I'm too old to be in the school. They were trying to send me to an alternative school. They just felt as though I could learn better there. And I had talked to Ms. K-- my principal at Southside Academy and I was telling her and she gave me a chance. I can do. I will make it right. I might not be in my uniform, but I'm in school every day. I ain't going to say on time, but I'm passing all my classes.

But it made me feel mad that they were trying to send me to a different school. It had me thinking that the school system was letting me down, was giving up on me. Ms. K-- kept telling me like, she's always telling me, "You can do." Like "You're not a bad child." My mother come up there for a parent/teacher conference - just tell my mother I'm not a bad child. I can do, just sometimes I get caught up in my ways.

But Ms. K--, I guess she thought I wasn't on the Southside level, like she thought I may be better off at an alternative setting. I could learn more, plus I need a lot of credits this year to graduate. But we was looking it over, me and Mr. M—[the assistant principal], and he just said as long as I pass all my classes I will graduate on time because at the end of the semester the classes switch.

I only want to say a good teacher should be kind, but I hope a good teacher's smart like when the child needs your help, you got to be there for them. You should treat them like they're your child when you're in a learning setting. When you come to work every day, your job is to teach us, to motivate us, to make sure we got it in our head and don't give up on us because we fail our math test or a quiz, a pop quiz we didn't know we had or forgot we had. I mean, we still are smart students. I don't think nobody is dumb. Some people lose their ways and they are caught up in the wrong crowd or just give up on their self, but how do you expect somebody to motivate you if you ain't going to motivate yourself? If you ain't going to believe in yourself, then can't nobody believe in you.

MCINTOSH

At this school, we only have four electives, that's it. It's only like three different electives. I liked it the way it was last year. It was eleven classes for one hour [each] and now it's like four classes for an hour and a half. It's not working. Because now, this is my day: I go to Algebra II, then I go to English II, then

I go to JROTC, then I go to science. Now, I'm only getting seven credits this year because last semester I had English II – I didn't fail it, but that's a year-round class. So if it was a regular school, I would get like nine credits a year, but here I'm only getting seven a year. Not to mention, if you fail a class, then things are going to be way worse. And it's only like four electives, so Spanish, you have to take Spanish at Southside. And like, at Poly [Polytechnical High School] they've got Chinese. My little brother, he goes to Poly and he can take Chinese. Russian. More options.

I feel like they rush the teachers. In certain classes - except for English and the classes we have year round - they rush the teachers. Like Algebra II, we be doing something today and a whole different thing tomorrow to get us ready for HSA and we only have a semester and if we fail this, then got to do it all over again next year and it's going to mess up the credits.

And another thing about school, like the class of 2010, when we have our class meetings, so far we have nothing done. We just got the colors and we just got the mascot. We don't have no prom, nothing about prom, no trips coming up. It's the fault of the president, kind of, like the class meetings that we go to, they don't have no order. Everybody's just talking. Teachers just sitting there. They don't care. And another thing, why do we meet like once a month? We need to meet like at least twice a month.

I think more people would pay their dues if they made it seem like they were strong on giving refunds. So, let's say I pay my dues for a trip, and it's a day before a trip I get into a fight and I can't go on a trip, I'm suspended. They say no refunds. I think people are just scared they just lost their money. I think that's why – so if they made a refund policy, then I think more people would pay too.

MIGUEL

I like that we only have four classes and it gives us less homework, but I don't like it because the classes are too long. I like my schedule because I go to Geometry, from Geometry I go to English II, from English II, JROTC, and from JROTC to Government. But the classes are too long and especially at the end of the day - Government, you know, the bell don't ring on time, and we got to get them buses, people got to go to work. You don't get too many buses in Cherry Hill. And there are just too much people in the classes. It's too packed and I don't like it.

And then summer school, $150 per class. That's just way overboard. I don't believe that you should pay for summer school, but I do believe that you should stay focused so you wouldn't have to go to summer school. But not making you pay because you messed up, you know. So I mean, really I do believe in second chances. The school system should give students a second chance, but if you've got a chance, take the chance and don't mess up on it. And you know, somebody told me if a teacher's giving you a break, take the break. Don't go ahead and mess it up. But $150 is too much. $25 a class, yeah. Or $30 a class.

As the school knows, we are the juniors coming up. And the juniors will be seniors. And come time for senior inauguration next year, they'll be passing the torch to us, and we don't have nothing planned out for inauguration. I think next year, what they're going to do is – I think all the teachers are going to get together and they're going to rush the eleventh grade class to pay their money. And my thing is, if the president ain't going to pay the money first and the vice president pay first and then all the officers pay and then the whole house pay, then I'm not going to touch my money. I've told the president if the president put hers in, I bet you other people would follow. Then we got to pay for cap and gown and all that other stuff.

And see, about the fundraiser, we planned for the tenth grade house to take a room and open up a school store. Well, let me tell you the school store was my idea. Miss Z--'s class just took the room back. It's crazy. Let me tell you the thing about this. This was last semester when we first got the tenth grade class together and I said we should do us a school store. And the school store thing got out and I guess Miss Z-- threw $500 in of her money and they started paying and I'm like, wow, we really did get this school store up and running and come to find out they say the money will be divided into every class. But the money isn't going anywhere right now because I don't even think the school store has opened up. And they just took our idea.

Then we try to do a basketball tournament –Miss K-- [school principal] said we could do it on this date, didn't even let us know we had to have a permit to hold the basketball tournament. Security, permission slips for the players to play from their moms. We had to have chaperones there. I mean, why give us the run around? And they say it shouldn't be during the school day. Got to be after school. That takes some of the incentive out because who wants to stay after school? If we did do it during the day, we wouldn't have to pay for a permit, we wouldn't have to pay for the school police. We'd have the chaperones.

They just don't want the tenth grade class to get fundraisers right now. But, come time for us to get in eleventh grade, all the teachers will be rushing us to get our money in. Why should we? We're trying to get our money now and you won't let us make no money. So, maybe we do a car wash or something in the summer. We all get together some day, hook the hose up, use public school water.

I'll come back next year – yeah, I'll go all the way up until twelfth [grade]. I would. I wouldn't want to go to another school, got to meet all new friends. Yeah, so, Southside ain't that bad. I'll be here.

Untitled

By Deinera

"Deinera A-- please report to the main office." It was only the third month of my second year in sixth grade and my principal was already calling my name. I walked into the hallway nervous, not sure what I had done. She walked me to her office and told me to take a seat and she would be right back with me, so I sat and waited patiently. She said she had two things she had to tell me. One was she wanted me to run an errand. Then she said by the time I got back my DR (suspension letter) would be ready. It really took me by surprise. I yelled, "Why am I getting a DR?" She said she would explain it to me when I came back. She handed me a stack of papers to take to the seventh grade teachers. I had totally forgotten about the DR when I heard that. My fear turned into happiness because I was finally going to see my last year friends, so I jumped right up and was on my way upstairs. As I hit their hallway it was so much different. The air was fresh, the walls were stainless, and even the floors were mopped and clean. This all came as a surprise to me. I didn't even know we had janitors. I felt like a lower class man.

The sixth graders ran hall, we wrote on walls, we poured water on the floors and we didn't listen to a word our teachers had to say. On the other hand the seventh graders walked in straight lines, they obeyed all rules, they were like an army, they could be beat physically but never mentally.

I saw all of my friends and they looked at me and turned their heads. I knew they saw me, but I didn't want to believe it. I yelled their names: "Kiera! Johnnie!, Jermaine!" The look they gave me as they walked into their classroom hurt me real bad.

They had disowned me. My best friends. The same friends that I failed for, the friends that I fought for, the friends I hooked class with, the same friends I got suspended for had disowned me and I wanted to cry. But I didn't; I had to be strong, not for my ego but for me. I refused to show them that they had hurt me. I refused to show them my weakness, that's just how I am. Then I got myself together, cleared my throat and walked into the first classroom. I spoke to the teacher. I guess I was loud because the whole class looked up and shushed me. So I yelled "shhh" right back. Some giggled, some mugged but I couldn't care less. I just wanted to hurry up and get out of there and get to my friend's class. I yelled to the class "bye" very sarcastically and walked out, then slammed the door behind me.

I walked into the next classroom and this one was silent. They were serious and I didn't understand why until I had seen their teacher. Ms. W- was her name; she was no joke. She had been working in the school system for fifteen years and never put up with nothing from her students. She had a face that had a permanent mug and she had scoliosis so her head was never above the hunch in her back. You would think she would quit her job after all that she puts up with – the cracks, the jokes - but she was just like the teacher from *The Skin I'm In*. She said she had been everywhere and had heard it all. There was nothing no one could say to hurt or break her. This might sound strange but I admired her. I quickly gave her the papers, not looking at her class. "Thank you," she replied and I hurried up out her class this time slowly shutting the door behind me.

Here it is, my friend's class. I was so excited. I fixed my shirt, looked at my shoes and rubbed my hair to make sure it was right, then I cleared my throat. I walked in and everyone looked up. I then waved to all the people I used to be with. Two out of sixteen waved back. As they waved, their teacher gave them this look and pointed and yelled, "Zero! Both of you."

The teacher then snatched the papers from my hand and said, "Thank you!" in a rude and ignorant way. I tried to let it go but I felt my insides bubbling. I then yelled, "I hate ignorant people!" "What?" she screamed back. I didn't recall studdering. She said that I was very disrespectful. I told her she had to "Give respect to get respect. My brother is two years old and he knows that. How you gonna teach if you didn't learn that?" as I walked out. She stood there with a startled look on her face.

I felt defeated. I might have won the argument but she did what she wanted. She broke me down; she knew that I was on contract and I was trying to get to the seventh grade and this could hold me back for good. I shut her door and stood outside of it to hear what she had to say. "See class, it's people like her. That's the same little girl that has no potential. The same girl you're gonna see bent over on the corner ten years from now. The same little girl that's gonna be here till she's twenty. She is a nobody and that's how he is going to be for the rest of her life." I stood there and listened to her say all those negative things about me. With those words it was like she took a knife and put it inside of me and twisted and turned it until I bled to death.

I felt dumb and I felt like everything she said was the truth and it hurt. She had hurt me but little did she know those words were motivation for me. It was soon time for classes to change so I hurried to the restroom to wipe my eyes. I walked out the bathroom and headed back to my floor. I walked into my principal's office. She looked at me and laughed. She could tell I had been crying because my eyes and cheeks were red. I was then handed my DR letter and it said that I was suspended for three days for cursing Ms. C- on the seventh grade floor.

I couldn't argue with her. That's when I realized it was a set up. She knew how those teachers and children would treat me. She knew they would tick me off and cause me to go off. She knew me well. I walked out of her office and went home.

I showed my mom the letter and walked straight to my room with no explanation. Not even five minutes later my mom bust into my room. She was yelling at me. Saying "Who do you think you are that you can come in the house three hours early and just hand me a suspension letter and just walk away? Does that sound right to you?"

"No" I said.

"We need to start over." She grabbed my arm and walked me outside. She then shut the door and left me on the porch to start off fresh. I put my key in the door. This time when I walked in the room I said to my mom as I handed her the letter, "Mom, I got suspended today."

"Why?" was her response. I began to tell her the story of how I was set up. "That all sounds bogus to me," is what I remember her yelling at me. I was sent to my room. I laid across my bed and read my pink carpet that read "No!" I couldn't stop thinking about how well that principal knew me and all that I went through that day. I just kept thinking three things: "Nobody," "the same little girl," and "ten years from now." I thought long and hard. I then realized that it was time to change.

The next couple of weeks I did nothing but work. I listened, I participated, I was focused and serious. A few things came my way that almost distracted me but I had a goal and I refused to become what these teachers thought I would. I felt that I deserved to be just like those seventh graders I knew. I had potential, I had dreams, I had goals, and I was very smart and talented. I knew that I would never be bent over on nobody's corner ten years from then. I learned to never second-guess talents or potentials. I learned that I was just as good as the next person. I worked long and hard and I waited for things to work out in my favor. I did get my promotion letter, then my mother decided that I needed a change from that school in order for me to succeed. I walked out of the school building that day and the sun was shining, the birds was singing and I felt wonderful. I fought a battle and I came out on top; I had **WON.**

Untitled

by William

(Derived from a sparkword activity in Ms. Stone's English 9 class)

My mother tell me everyday
Keep your head up and go to school
The shit that I do is making me look like a fool
On (by) the skin of my teeth I passed
I'm always gonna stay so fly over and over again
But if I don't wake up 10th grade is gonna be my best friend
Fuck! That shit can't happen
But if it do, fuck school
I'm just gonna start trappin
Psych fuck that it's so hard for me to do
I won't let all the mother fuckers who downed my dream come true
This some bullshit
I gotta have a diploma in my life
This shit might feel like forever but imma make school my wife
I gotta finish this shit so the world can see
A high school diploma and a college degree
In this world you not nothing but a black nigger
This shit killin me like a gun wit two triggers
I'm good though, I'm never gonna be stuck
Be my brother role model but I still don't give a fuck.

3

FRIENDS AND ENEMIES

*I've got some good company and I've got some bad company.
I'm not going to disown them, but if it came down to it, I would leave
them alone. If it came down to what I've got to do in life.*
LAJUANE

*A good friend has to be trustworthy.
You can't have a friend that lies to you a lot. They have to be reliable
and you have to rely on them to help you with problems.*
GAGE

DEAIRRA

A characteristic of a good friend to me is someone who's devoted to the friendship besides you. I've been in so many situations where I'm the best friend to everybody, but where's my best friend? I'm always there to listen and give advice, but I have no one to talk to and receive advice from. So a characteristic of a good friend is someone who can listen, someone who's not wrapped up in themselves or someone else, as though they can't spend time with a friend.

GAGE

Listening to Gage. *Gage was shy and quiet as a ninth grader. He had admirers but he was too quiet even for the bolder girls. However, he didn't shy away from participating in discussion or engaging a classmate in a civil debate. He was reserved. His writings are insightful and revealing. There is no shame. He shares intimate details about himself and that encourages others to dig deep.*

A good friend has to be trustworthy. You can't have a friend that lies to you a lot. They have to be reliable and you have to rely on them to help you with problems. Like I have a friend and I always talk to him about my problems and he gives me the best advice that he can give me as a friend.

SARAI

I like being on my own because you really can't trust anybody anymore. And if you try to trust somebody, that's just going to make you mad and a little sadder. Like the girl next door. I called her my best friend but she really wasn't my best friend. She did things to discourage me and stuff, like when I did good things in my life, she'd get mad and say a lot of little funny things about me and I didn't like it.

I don't have no good friends. No good friends. D-- she's a good friend, but she's not a good, good friend. Just the other day –we was hanging together – me, her and J-- and we stopped at somebody's house and J-- said she had to go to the bathroom. And I was like, "Come on D–, we got to go, J-- got to go to the bathroom." And D– wouldn't come on. She kept saying "Hold on, hold on" and the girl peed on herself. And D– gonna laugh. And I didn't really think it was funny and J– started crying. And I was like, "See, see?" I was mad. That's what triggered me. I was like now I really don't have no good friends because I thought she's nice, she's smart, and she's cool, but she's really not a good friend and all my other friends they definitely wasn't a good friend.

LAJUANE

Everybody says choose the company wisely. You got to lose some friends and you're going to gain friends too. Every situation is not good for you. I've got some good company and I've got some bad company. But I know that's just school friends. I'm not going to disown them, but if it came down to it, I would leave them alone. If it came down to what I've got to do in life. They not going to be here forever, and even if they is - like when people say how when you graduate you're not going to see half of the people you went to school with, even the little bit of people that you do still keep in contact with. They're still going to start their own families and live their own life. It ain't like you can go to them and ask them stuff.

LAKEDA

I think society has gotten a lot worse now. I have been watching the news lately and in schools kids been getting shot and stabbed. So I think it has gotten a lot worse because back in the day you never really heard too much about a child being shot or stabbed in school. It was always an issue where it wasn't enough textbooks or the bathrooms needed different materials, tissues, stuff like that, but it was never a child being shot or killed.

My thought is that it may be because of peer pressure. I see a lot of kids - for example in my school - a lot of kids do what they see their friends doing just to fit in so they try to be cool just as they see their friends being cool. They feel like well, maybe if I smoke weed because she's smoking weed or he's smoking weed, then I'll look cool like they look cool. Maybe if I be in this gang, I can look cool because my friend's in this gang and they look cool. But what they don't know is, it's going to make their life a lot worse than what it already is. They just put their life in jeopardy.

Sometimes I honestly do feel that type of pressure. I have friends, but I don't have a lot of friends. I'm more so the type of person that likes to stay to myself because I feel that I can get a lot more accomplished if I stays to myself. But I have ran across a lot of people that have tried to influence me to do a lot of different things.

DEINERA

The thing I didn't like about school was the peers. The peers. I'm not saying they was the reason I slacked, but by me knowing everybody, by being well known, they was just a huge distraction. By me knowing and being known by everybody, this person wanted me to do this, this person wanted me to do that. Instead of me saying "No, *that's* what I should be doing." I did what I wanted to do instead of what needed to be done.

The difference between me and my friends were they were a lot smarter. They had fun, but they got their work done. So they got to do the same things at the end of the day and still passed their classes. Me, I was just all fun. Class just wasn't important to me.

A good friend is somebody that don't – or won't - allow you to do wrong or influence you to do bad. A good friend won't talk about you behind your back or if they feel as though you're doing something bad or wrong or that you shouldn't be doing, they'll let you know about it.

If you pull me to the side and say hey, you're cutting up, get it together, then we cool, but if you want to point me out – it depends on the way you say it. If you come say, "You're young, you doing this, you're doing that," then we're going to have a problem. If you just pull me to the side and [have a] mature one-on-one, then I might consider it.

It takes so much to build a friendship and you can just lose it at the snap of a finger. It's so easy to lose a friend in high school when certain people that see your relationship, they admire your relationship and want your relationship. And therefore tries their hardest to break it apart. Then, you got some friends that will give into the hype of the jealous people and it will affect the friendship, and then you've got the strong ones that try to keep it together. So it's very easy to lose a friend in high school.

4

IDENTITY AND INTERESTS

If somebody tells me, "Oh, you're not going to be nothing in life"- watch. I'm going to be the best nurse or pediatrician in the world. You will see it on the news and making money. Watch. Everybody's like "Tarena, you so confident, you've got so much potential in life." Like, I know. I know. **TARENA**

I want people to listen to things that I say. The words that I say are not meaningless. They all equal up to something, you know, whether it has to do with your mother not listening or the way you feel about certain things. **ASHLEY**

I don't understand how people just grow patience. I'm ADHD. Look what I'm like. I'm always running around, bouncing around. ADHD makes my life fun. I think that people that be slower, calmer, they don't have fun. **DELORIS**

LAKEDA

I was retained when I was in the fourth grade. It has affected me because I have learned from it. I have more self-esteem and confidence for myself and it is helping me become a better person in life. The best piece of advice that anyone has given me is from my fourth grade teacher. I had a big issue with my self-esteem and always giving up and she has always told me to never give up and always say I can and not I can't. She actually wasn't just there for me during the fourth grade year. She actually was a teacher of mine and as time went on she seen the type of child that I was. She could see that I had potential and I *had* potential, but at the same time I didn't know how to put forth all the effort that I could because I was always doubting myself because I'm not good at taking tests. So when I failed the test, I always said well, I'm not good enough. I can't do this. I can't do that.

But she turned my can'ts into cans and as time go on, I continue to take tests and my grades are improving. Yes, I still need help, but my grades are improving and I don't say I can't anymore. I don't doubt myself. I still stay in touch with her and she still gives me advice and she still say when she see me, "Lakeda, what do I always tell you?" And I say that "I can, not I can't." And it puts a smile on her face.

Life can be hard and I just had an assignment to do in my English II class actually. And I actually wrote about me being retained and I like to write about that a lot. Actually, I had to write an ECR [extended constructed response] because I feel like it had so much of a big impact on my life. Kids read about it and saw that I went through so much - that I have had the opportunity to be placed in my right grade, but I choose not to because I feel like even though I know I belong in the eleventh grade and I'm in the tenth grade, I feel like this is where I belong. This is who I am even though I know that I should be in the right grade. But I actually like it. It's a lot better. I've learned from it.

TARENA

If somebody tells me, "Oh, you're not going to be nothing in life" - watch. I'm going to be the best nurse or pediatrician in the world. You will see it on the news and making money. Watch. Everybody's like "Tarena, you so confident, you've got so much potential in life." Like, I know. I know.

Me and my little brother is just alike. He's kind of crazy. People always telling him you're not going to make it in this world and keep going on and on. He buckled down and passed all his classes with an 80 and above. He was on the honor roll two years in a row. And he's proving everybody wrong.

SARAI

I worry a lot. I worry a lot and sometimes I cry. I worry a lot about everything, like am I going to live to the next day? Is something going to happen to me or my family members any day? Am I going to have to go to a funeral? I just worry a lot, a lot. Then, just the other day, I found two gray strings in my hair. I wanted to pull it out. I wanted to pull it out so bad! But I left them in. I left them in there because my mother says they're lucky.

Just the other day I was on the computer and I was looking at skulls, what are skulls and what does it mean. And it was saying that skulls are the sign of death, and you know how people wear the skulls and stuff – they wear the shirts, they have the skull shoes that have skulls on it and it's a sign of death. People are wearing it a lot and they don't understand that it's really a sign of death. And it's devils and demons and stuff.

And just the other day my cousin had bought some shoes and she looked at them and she was like, oh, they look so cute. Then one day we was just sitting there and she looked at them and she was like "Oh my gosh" and she threw it and she didn't know that there was a skull inside of them, like inside the shoe. And she didn't know. She was like – it must have snuck in the house, and I was like yeah, because I didn't see the skulls either. And a lot of people don't believe that the devil is real, but I do and I believe that God is real. And I believe everything in His word and stuff. And I read the Bible a lot and I try not to cuss and stuff. I really do. I try really hard not to cuss and do the wrong things to my life because I want to be successful.

I haven't always been this way. I was bad. I was cussing – I really wasn't that bad, but I cussed and I did bad things. I cussed a lot and stuff. I got in trouble. I never really got in trouble with school. I've always been good at school, but I got in trouble a few times. I got in trouble one time because I cut the extension cord while it was plugged up. I got a beating for that. I got in trouble one time because I lost my phone. I really didn't get in a lot of trouble a lot.

DELORIS

I don't have patience. If somebody's doing something and I feel as though I could do it better – move. Let me do it. Even if it's like something I'm not supposed to be doing. No, watch out. I don't have patience period. Like my friend, she walks really slow and I really get mad. Like, come on! I really get mad. Like, when I be in the bank, and it be a long line, I'll leave. I will wait until the next day to go, or the next hour.

I don't understand how people just grow patience. I'm ADHD. Look what I'm like. I'm always running around, bouncing around – I just know I got it. ADHD makes my life fun. I think that people that be slower, calmer, they don't have fun. I don't think they have fun. I'd be like what are you doing – just what are you doing?

Sometimes I get down. When my feelings really, really hurt. Or if I have a whole bunch of stuff going on and I can't do nothing about it. But I get over it. Maybe in the next hour, make me laugh or something. If there's nothing I can do, there's nothing I can do.

ASHLEY

I can get most of my thoughts out and my feelings in my poetry. I really started when I was in the sixth grade, but it started off with little songs and whatever when I was in the fifth grade, which turned into poetry, which later turned into rap, which is the spoken word. So, it was like, it was so special to me. I don't know why. And sometimes I have my doubts, like I'm not good at writing poetry or whatever because I see other people that are better than me.

I get excited when I read my poetry out loud because - it's like other people, they're not listening. They're not listening, which goes right to the title [of this book]. They're not listening, and so I just want people to listen. I don't just write poetry just to write it. I write it for myself at times, but it's like I want people to listen to things that I say. The words that I say are not meaningless. They all equal up to something, you know, whether it has to do with your mother not listening or the way you feel about certain things. I'm not the only person who feels this way, so I know that when I read my poetry, other people will connect with me gradually.

I have a poem that I thought that most people would connect to. Some people do feel this way, but I think, most of all, I feel this way. I have read it to my class, to my family, and I think they really – as a matter of fact, I ***know*** that they really know what I'm saying when I read it. Yeah, like they know - like wow! Like that's really deep.

The one I have to read, the one that's really deep is called, "I Love My Body." I think this is really good for teenagers, because if you really sit there and you think about it, most people don't have certain parts. Some people don't have a leg and some people don't have an arm. I think about that all the time. Some people who don't have legs or arms, they feel bad. But some people don't have eyes. And it goes on and on and on. I think it is really good for them to think about because you've got to think about it. We take things for granted. We take life for granted. Seriously, we take life for granted. We sit there – and you can't tell me that one time you haven't sat there and got so mad and just thought man, I just can't – I wish I would die. Nobody in this world can tell me they haven't got that mad before. All right, this is called, "I Love My Body."

> I love the way my curves run wild
> And the complexion of my skin, Hershey brown.
> I love the way my smile goes in the sun,
> How I can light up the room with just one of them.
> I love the way my dimples go round
> Like a semi-sweet circle mixed up with caramel.
> I love my body and the features that it holds,
> Eyes like diamonds, ears like gold.
> I'm loving me and my skin's so soft,
> Nails so natural, long and all.
> I love the rise of my two lemon drops -
> Never falling, always on top.

How can you tell me I'm not unique?
How can you tell me I'm not fit to be a queen?
How can you tell me I'm not good enough?
I'm not a small figure that only half can love.
Why do you question my gratitude?
Am I just too overconfident or am I just being too rude?
Well, let me tell you something, I'm unpredictable.
You should be proud to be receiving my love,
My candlelight and Hershey kisses.
Love not in a box but I fit like a glove.
I'm not a present but a blessing in your life
Because the features that I hold have no price.

The thing this poem shows is that you should love who you are. Long nails and all. When I describe myself, I don't try to lie, I just try to keep it real. I don't have this, so why would I put that? That's not loving yourself. You gotta love yourself, no matter what. You might not have no hair. You still gotta love yourself. I can make a poem out of that. It just comes naturally. Like when I was sitting there crying because I thought, you know, I'm not pretty. Why does this person like me or this person? I question it sometimes. If somebody likes me, I question it. I shouldn't question it. You should already know. I shouldn't have to sit there and question it.

The reason I question it is because I have low self-esteem sometimes. But I haven't had low self-esteem in like the longest time. I think when I read my poems people think that I have low self-esteem. But really I haven't had it in the longest time. But I write it. When you can write it – when you can just sit there and you can write it when you don't feel that way at that certain time and you can actually make it sound so real - I think that is a gift.

I have more poems in here [her notebook]. Sometimes I write poems and some people in the class – I know they can connect to it. But they don't say nothing. You can tell that they connect with it. And Ms. Stone, she tells us, to write poems when we're in class. We do write poems in her class a lot.

This is called "Running Down A Grown Man." I love this poem. I wrote it in class. We had to do something about football and I was thinking, oh my God, I hate football. I was thinking about who do I know who can play really good football. And I didn't say nobody. They're in my class. They're in Ms. Stone's class. You'll see them when you go in the classroom. But, he never knew. He said, "That poem's about me, isn't it?" I was like, "No."

> I know about a boy that stands so tall,
> Can run down anyone and do touchdowns in football.
> He's very unique in the style that he has -
> Strong calf muscles, mouth like a laugh.
> It's funny, you know, an athlete undiscovered,
> Soon to be a black brother, one of our brothers.
> Never discreet, complex look,
> Complains about reading but loves football books
> And believes that nappy natural is the way to go.
> He has transformed into a man instead of a kid -
> Strong as a door that cannot be opened,
> As smart as a book when his mind is open.
>
> I know about a boy that stands so tall,
> Can run down anyone and do touchdowns in football.
> May not know how much I believe in him
> And not just a black man, but another living dream.
> Because if he tries hard, then we all can succeed.

My poetry is a part of me. It's always going to be a part of me. I really want to write poetry right now, but I can't think of nothing. It's like don't force it. It'll come. And then it finally comes. Words come to me like, you could be saying to me right now and it will just pop right in my head. The whole poem, and I'll just start writing real quick. And it's amazing. Like my mother, she'll talk to me and she'll say one word, just one thing, just one specific word, just a sentence like, "I feel alone." She never said that though, but if she said "I feel alone," I would just be thinking, I feel alone. And it will just come to me and I'll just want to hurry up and go upstairs and get so excited about it. I get excited reading my poetry. I don't know why - it's just always been there for me.

    Before it was songs. I would come up with my own melody in my head and then it was just like lyrics just come out – they come out like poetry. One day I was going to the school to pick up my brothers and one little girl, she was playing with her Barbie doll. And I was thinking, hey, what if one of those musicians turned into a Barbie doll? I was just thinking that would be a pretty cool idea. I saw a piece of cardboard on the ground and I had a pen in my pocket. So I was just writing it. I just went home and I was just writing it in a book.

TYESHA

Listening to Tyesha. *Tyesha is loud, even when she is close. You wouldn't believe a body so small could be so loud. She tells it like it is and is not ashamed. Her main hobby is sleeping. During a class discussion Tyesha revealed intimate details about her life. She shared about a decision she didn't get to make.. She cries and the class listens sympathetically. Her secret remained in class.*

    I'm funny. I get my sense of humor from my mother. She try to be funny, she try to be, she try. I was quiet, but I'm not quiet no more. They was taking my kindness for weakness. And then, my voice is little so I got to be loud so they can hear me. So now I just be loud. And I like myself. People don't like me but I don't care. So I like it.

In my spare time I go to sleep at my house. I've got a sleeping problem. I can sleep all day if I had to. I go to work at Ja-Ja's at Security Mall. I make $6.15 minimum wage. It needs to go up. I spend my money on clothes and shoes - and to pay for this prom and stuff that's coming up.

AARON S.

I work at Martin's West. I get stuff ready for the chefs. I clean up after the chefs and I cook food sometimes when they ain't got time enough to do it. I just fry chicken, bake chicken, everything. I do a lot. Work is just like at school, you got to watch your language. I don't know, I guess it's because I'm coming to get my check. I know they ain't having it – they ain't having it at all - you got to come there right. You got to. Just like I always say at Southside. You got to come right. Say I see a female at work. I might say that I'm attracted, like, "Look at her, look at shorty right there." Well, but if I'm outside on a corner with my home boys, six or seven of my home boys, and I see a female that I'm attracted to, I might say "Oh, look at that bitch."

MELISSA

In my spare time, I sit at my computer. MySpace, MyCrib, E-box, MSN, Yahoo. Then Potspace. And I make bracelets. I made my watch[band].

MIGUEL

Officer Kevin Robinson came to my school in sixth grade, and they were talking about the different programs to get kids off the street. He went around the class and asked everyone what they wanted to be in life and me, I always wanted to be a police officer and he came, talked to me after the class and he was like, if you really want to be a police officer, you can join my program, Explorer Program.

So I joined his program and I've been in his program for six years now. We do a drilling ceremony. We do different kind of trainings on gangs, gang-related information. Then we do practicums, like they train us on what do you do when you're ready to pull over a car. It's called traffic stops. We do burglary - he'll bring a police car and we practice in the parking lot. He uses the lights and siren and stuff. We go out in the summertime and do the Safe Zone that Sheila Dixon started up. We do those and we do block parties, community events, McGruff.

Officer Robinson is someone I look up to. He's not too much of a street cop. He told us the last time he arrested someone was five years ago and he only used his gun round about five times in his nineteen-year career. I really look up to him because he got the time for us. Busy as a police officer could be, he's the one that's got the time for us. Like, on the weekends, we go out to his house and play games with his kids and just have fun.

I can count many adults that give time, lot of time, lot of time. I got another group that I goes to and another person I look up to. His name is Rob Benson. He used to be a police officer, but he said that he didn't want to see kids be arrested anymore, so what he did was he got a ministry group going on and now he's the pastor and started his own church and he started different clubs and youth groups like Men of Valor and Campus Life. They have a headquarters, Youth for Christ headquarters and they all work inside Youth for Christ and they started a Howard County club and Anne Arundel club and all that other stuff. I'm in the Police Explorers and through them I'm in the Baltimore City Men of Valor.

HEATH

Listening to Heath. *Heath is the only Caucasian boy in the class for two years in a row. He is an intellectual and he is quiet. He watched his classmates and knew they "just don't get it." I told him that he should participate more in class and share his ideas. "They don't care, why should I?" He made me think about the saying "casting your pearls among the swine." He would talk to me before or after class about his ideas. We would have class before class. I allowed it because I understood. Kids can be cruel, especially at Southside, and especially if you are bright and don't hide it.*

Heath was an awesome writer and avid reader. By the tenth grade he opened up a little. He participated more, shared his ideas more. This year, his classmates respected his intelligence and many times sought to complete group assignments with him. However, he shied away because he knew that working in a group was more trouble that it was worth.

Books have made me who I am. Any kind of book. I love books absolutely and I think because I read books at such an early age, it's made me who I am. I love reading poetry, everything. And because of that, my vocabulary has increased, you know, all of that. I think the government should put more money towards books. More libraries. Libraries that are now in better condition, expanding what they can have and updating the Baltimore City reading list. It's ridiculous because it's full of nothing but black empowerment books. I'm like, that's really stupid. You need some Tolkien, some T.S. Eliot, everything in there. And it's focused on these black empowerment books because they think everyone in Baltimore City is black. And I'm like, that's not true. And although they should have the choice of those books, you should have a wide range of books that teaches everything.

I buy my books at bookstores, Barnes & Noble. My parents give me the money. My dad's a big reader. I've got this humongous book collection. I'm reading a Dean Koontz book called **Seize the Night.** Oh, he's got the most twists and turns – he goes into science and religion and politics all at once and he molds them together into just one plot line that's just – it holds you. And I read Dan Brown. I read all of the *Lord of the Rings*. I liked them. Another of my favorite ones is Tracy Hickman and Margaret Weiss. They do this series called **Dragon Lance**. I love it because it's so articulate and then I read this one where it was just really German origin and it let me see a lot of the German influence in the languages. Because I think it's all – it's amazing how our language is built up off of all these other languages. They took a bunch of it and you have a whole new language. And because I see all the Latin-based roots and the German roots, and stuff like that. I think that's amazing too.

I've already written a bunch of books myself. I just write them and then I go back and I reread and tweak them and put them away. My dad's been encouraging me to write this one I was trying to write and I just sit there and lately I've been trying. I love books that don't explain the plot to you but rather just throw you into it and you have to catch onto it. Otherwise, you're going to get left behind. I like books like that, so I always try to start off my books like that. And I had this one – actually I wrote a really cool short story that you should read.

It's called *Tree Epiphany* where it's about a tree. The tree obviously has thought it's alive and he doesn't realize why he's a tree and whether or not he should be a tree and then he's kind of like saying "Is somebody going to come along and tell me what I'm going to be?" And he's like, why would I wait for someone to tell me? Why can't I just be what I want to be? And he goes through this whole real life realization in five minutes and then he's so proud of himself for coming to this and then a lumberjack comes along and says, "You're going to be paper" and then the last thing – the last sentence of the story is ***he started the chain saw.***

Tree Epiphany

By Heath

The tree just stood there doing nothing,
bothering noth¬ing.
He had no idea why he was a tree
Or why he was there for that matter.
He didn't remember being a tree.
He didn't remember being anything at all.
So why the feeling that he shouldn't be a tree?
Was he even a he?
Was there any way to check if a tree was a he?
Why should he be a he-tree?
Was someone gonna come along and tell him what to be?
If no one was gonna tell him what to be
why be anything at all?
Maybe because he wanted to be something.

"You're Not Listening"

And why would he wait for someone to come along
and tell him what to be?
If he wanted to be something then he would
be what he wanted to be.
He was proud of this realization.
So proud that he didn't notice the lumberjack
come up to him.
Then he did look down at the man
that was so small compared to him,
Wondering what he was.
The lumberjack looked up to the tree and said
"You're gonna be paper."
Then he started the chainsaw.

5

SEX AND MARRIAGE

A man should be able to stand on his own. I just feel as though boys, like we powerful, like we stronger than a female. Females, they are unique. You're right, they is some females stronger than men, but I feel as though females bring men up in a way. Like a male can give you tips, but a female, they put you through life. **CHOC**

The most significant thing that has ever happened to me was when I first got my heart broken. We was going together for a year and three months and for that long time, I thought he loved me.... For a real long, long time, I didn't get over it. I missed two days of school and my mother tried to do this stuff like take me shopping and stuff like that.
BRITTNEY

Marriage is a waste of yourself because when you get married, what's yours is his and what's his is yours. So, if you get a divorce [and] you make more money than him, you're going to have to pay him. **MADISEN**

TYESHA

Guys like me and that make the girls mad. The girls be mad. I don't have a boyfriend and I don't want one. I had one and I do want one, but not right now.

I don't want to get married because once that ring's on your finger, you can't do nothing. And I like to party, so I don't want to get married. I'm going to have kids. I don't want to get married because when you're married you can't do nothing. I'm afraid I'm going to have to kill my husband because he might cheat. My mother raised her children on her own and she didn't mind. I'm independent now, so I don't need no boy to help me.

MELISSA

Listening to Melissa. *Melissa is quiet and refuses to participate, complete assignments and most times even come to class. Tenth grade proved to be different. She smiled more, came to class more, and managed to complete some assignments. Like the others, Melissa opened up in tenth grade.*

I have a boyfriend. Right now he's in jail. I have no idea why. I asked his mom. This is the second time in jail in the last two weeks. He was in a group home, then he got out, then he snuck over to my house and I snuck him into my bedroom. I like the bad boys.

JANAE

Teenage girls look at boys because they're not getting love at home and by them not getting love at home, they're probably vulnerable and gullible and so whatever guys tell them, they're going to listen to it and be real retarded and think that it's true.

I hate when a boy tells me I'm pretty. Not because I know that I'm pretty, but because I feel like the only reason you're telling me that - even now with Jordan - I don't like him telling me I'm pretty because I feel that you're just telling me so you can do it to me. When he tells me I'm pretty I really hate him. If somebody in my family tells me I'm beautiful, then I might be fine. But just for a guy that's trying to mess with me, to tell me that, then I just don't like it. They're trying to get something from me. That's just how I feel.

From all the men that are in my life, I have not once met a man or a boy that did not cheat. And so I just now, after being in a relationship, my recent relationship, I just look at relationships like what's the point? I don't want to get married. I think marriage is a waste of money.

I don't even want to have kids because I just don't want to be connected to that same person - like right now I say "I love you, that's my baby." I do feel like I love him, but I still don't want to have no kids by him because I'm going to have to be with him, not even until my children are eighteen, but forever. And I just don't want it.

There is nothing you can tell a teenager to make them not want to have sex. You can say it hurts. You can say it will kill you. You can say anything you want. It's not going to make them not have sex. But you should tell them the experience and they can go from there. But there's nothing you can do to make somebody not want to do something.

I don't have too many regrets in my life, but I still wish I could go back and change the fact that I did have sex. Just that I had sex at all because it's nothing like – yeah it feel good but it's nothing that you need. And me and my little cousin are not speaking right now because she started having sex, and I talked to her for like days and I really was talking to her like overnight, please don't have sex. It's not worth it. Once you do it to him, he's not going to want to go out with you. There's no point in doing it. And she still started having sex.

DEINERA

Girls are way more mature than boys. I cannot explain it. Boys in high school and girls in high school are like two different things. The boys like to clown around and play, but the girls want a serious note, try to graduate and get out of there. So that's the difference, the maturity level.

AARON S.

I got a girlfriend. Keep me focused and make me go to work every day and make me do what I got to do. It's hard being sixteen, with a girl. You got to be right. (Laughs) You got to be right. It just makes me do what I got to do, just like my mother and my father.

A man got to be a man and a woman got to be a woman because there's a difference. It's a big difference. Matter of fact because at the end of the day, the man got to bring the bacon home. He got to bring the bacon home. He got to do a lot of physical stuff, like he got to go out and get a job. He got to take care of home. He got to make sure home is right. That's who I was looking at growing up. That's why I wanted to bring the bacon home. Not my mother, my father. I wanted my mother to wash my clothes and make sure I had my lunch ready for school tomorrow.

So yeah, the man bring the bacon home. He make sure everybody straight. Make sure you got your shoes, your new shoes and your school stuff. Make sure you have everything. A man that has sons or children or young males in his life to show them how to be a man. Not too many of my home boys even have father figures. That's why they do what they do. That's why they go outside with guns to protect their self or sell crack or dope every day because they didn't have a male figure in their life. And I don't look at a female as being a housewife or something like that. I don't think a female should have to do nothing like that, but more power to females who do be single mothers.

DELORIS

Boys stink. All of them are losers. All of them trifling. They all got kids or they're just trifling, want to play everybody. I'll probably get married, yeah, but no, not right now.

BRITTNEY

Listening to Brittney. *Brittney is full of drama and if she is in trouble the tears can roll at the drop of a nickel. She seems to be very sensitive. However, you have to have a keen eye and a cynical mind to see through her. She could easily manipulate you into feeling sorry for her and maybe not calling her father. She is bright, kind and at the age where boys are of all importance. She lives with her father and loves him dearly. She cares about what he thinks of her, though not so much because she fears him or she thinks she will get in trouble. His opinion and view of her is the most* *important thing. It even supersedes boys.*

The most significant thing that has ever happened to me was when I first got my heart broken. It hurt me because I really loved that boy and he really hurt my heart. Here's how it worked. I loved to be with him and he left me for somebody else he wanted to be with. It was upsetting. We was going together for a year and three months and for that long time, I thought he loved me. He'd tell me that he did, but then one day he broke up with me and I was so sad. He did it nicely. He said, "We need space." But I was crying. I didn't want him to say the rest. I just hung up. And then I just started crying.

And then for a real long, long time, I didn't get over it. I was stressed out. I missed two days of school and my mother tried to do this stuff like take me shopping and stuff like that. But it's not going to work because I got my heart broken. Sometimes I still think about him. I was fifteen. It was when I was in the eighth grade.

I liked his face. His eyes. It was great! He was so cute! And he was so sweet. But, at the same time, he could be controlling. He'd be like he could talk to another girl, but I can't talk to another boy. "Don't be with no other boy!" Saying stuff like that. I liked it.

I just thought he was my lesson. We broke up before. But that time, I broke up with him. And I don't think it hurt him. And then he wanted to get back with me. And then he broke up with me and my heart was broken because I gave him a second chance and he still broke my heart.

His name was Javonne. If I saw him again, I wouldn't go to him. I would get my friends. I wrote to him on myspace. He be reading them and don't respond. I call him and when he answers the phone, I hang up. I just want to hear his voice and then I hang up. Sometimes when I call I be wanting to say hi, but I don't want him to get smart with me or something. Hang up because he get smart with me, then it really gets emotional. He made it hard for me to trust other boys. I'm more suspicious now. With my boyfriend now. "You better not be over some girl's!" That's how I am. And he made me like that.

There are big differences between boys and girls. Yeah, because boys – if they like a girl – I feel as though if they really care about a girl, they don't want to show it in front of their friends. They don't want their friends to think they're stuck on a girl and stuff like that. And a girl might – she wants you to express your feelings to her around your friends to see how it is and stuff like that. Like, if you say you love me on the phone, why can't you say you love me in front of your friends or something like that?

And then boys always think that they can have a girlfriend and talk behind the other girl's back. They crazy! They are really crazy.

I was dating this older boy, he was seventeen; I'm fifteen; he was seventeen. And then, now I'm going with a fourteen year-old and he's treating me so much better than the seventeen year old. So I'm looking like, wow, I gotta go back to the younger ages to get what I want.

But the fourteen-year-old – he plays too much. He just plays too much. He doesn't know when to stop. He just plays and plays. But he treats me better than the seventeen-year-old. He spends time on me. He goes to church with me.

He better not flirt with other girls. I would just tell him you better not let me catch you flirting with other girls. I'm going to kill you. I'm not worried about her. I'm worried about you, because you probably told her you don't have a girlfriend.

I wouldn't want a boy to change up because then you wouldn't like them as much as you did when you met them. They just need to change their ways, the way they think. They just do dumb stuff, like they're not going to get caught. They date two people at the same time, lie and cheat.

It probably bugs boys that a girl always thinks a boy is cheating on her. Because if you don't really talk about that in your relationship, then I feel that your relationship is going to last longer because he feels as though "She trusts me." "I'm not going to do nothing to hurt her." But if I know for a fact [that a boy is cheating], I'm going to say something. I told my boyfriend if I find out he's cheating on me, I'm going to kill him. I'm not playing with him. I'm going to kill him.

Like yesterday - I cannot remember so I can't say that he didn't say nothing [to me], but he was talking to a girl. I can't stop him from talking to girls. But I just knew this boy didn't say hi to me. He called me when I got home. I said, "Why didn't you say hi to me?" He said, "I did say hi to you. What are you talking about?" I said "Oh." I just thought he didn't. It broke my nerves. If you can't act the same way when you're with me by yourself and when you're with your friends, then don't say nothing to me at all because you're phony. Boys is phony. When they like you for real, really like you, they don't try and show it in front of their friends because they don't want their friends think they are some kind of pimp.

I just want to say, why can't you all just settle down and pick this one girl? There are just some freaky girls that just want to mess with people's boyfriends, just to have sex and stuff like that.   So that's mainly why everybody's relationships fail because it's always some girls that's got to ruin them. They know that this boy's got a girlfriend, but they don't care. They just want sex with him. They make it hard to trust other boys. Like if a boy broke my heart now, I wouldn't run and jump right into another relationship. And if a boy said he wanted to talk to me, then I would tell him that I don't want it because I don't want to go through it again. How will I know he won't treat me the same way? Because I just got my heart broken and I don't want it to happen again.

All girls are not faithful. They cheat. They do the same thing that boys do. Some boys, most boys will stay with one girl. It's always something that messes up in the relationship. In a teenage relationship anyway. People are going to go through that. And then you've got to realize that you're not tied to nobody while you're in high school. You're not married. So, you got to give people their space.

I'm not getting married any time soon. I'm getting married when I'm twenty-five. I want to be a model. And then from that, I want to be a computer scientist. And when I do that, I'll get a good job and get married and have a family. But right now, I'm not worried about nothing like that. Some teenage girls, they're in love now and they want to hurry and rush into things. But I don't – that's not the way to go for me. I was raised better than that. And some girls are having babies and stuff. Then they're tied to their baby's father.

My father was telling me to choose right because he knows how boys is because he used to be one. He just wanted to sex girls and he says you know how boys is so you just choose wisely. And then my mother, she just keeps telling me to talk to her about all my relationships and be open with her. But I ain't talk to her about everything because she run around.

CHOC

Girls got special features, you know. They classy, different than a boy. A man should be able to stand on their own, but females also. I just feel as though boys, like we powerful. I feel as though like we stronger than a female. I feel as though females, they are unique. You're right, they is some females stronger than men, but I feel as though females bring men up in a way. My mother she more supportive. Yeah, females more supportive, like a male can give you tips, but a female, they put you through life. My mother will give me more support than my father for real. My father wasn't never in my life for real, and that affects me, like I'm a man.

MALCOLM

Listening to Malcolm. *In a word, Malcolm is hilarious! He is kind, outgoing and humorous. He was in love with Tori. "Ms. Stone, that girl is smart. I love her. That is the kind of girl I need in my life." He would walk by my door many times just to wave at Tori and blow kisses. She rolled her eyes and assumed the boy was crazy.*

He wears his hair in squarely parted plaits that hung down to his shoulders. He wears a set of gold fronts on his teeth. At first glance Malcolm looks intimidating but his smile would dissipate any fear. He played football and worked two jobs in order to help out at home. "Church" he would shout if he agreed with a classmate. "Sex is like church. All you hear is clappin' and shoutin' and people still come." The class roared. I have to admit—I laughed too. He was funny. He had a lot of challenges in his life but he was in school everyday and worked two jobs to help maintain his household.

The woman's ovary is a crystal ball. That is true. I got it all figured out. The women's ovary is a crystal ball. They can see the future, because they're always right. The men always think they're wrong, but in the end they're always right. My mother told me something bad's going to happen to you one day and it happened.

TARENA

Once I get myself situated, like I'm out of college, got a job that's well being for me to benefit my kids, then I would have kids. I do not want to be driving with the MTA [Baltimore's bus system] for the rest of my life. I would like to get a car. If I want to have kids, I'm not going to be dragging my kids on the bus.

I'm going to be better than my parents. That's all I can say. Like I'm always going to be there for my child. You got some parents that the father's not around and they have a step-father. Don't you know how some kids try to tell their parents if their step-father is molesting them and the parents don't believe them? So I'm going to believe anything my child say to a certain point. If I think they are lying – other than that, I'm going to believe my child.

And, I know when parents beat them, it's okay to like pop them on the hand or smack them on the butt, but when it gets to the point when you're beating them in their face, I'm not doing that to my child. Beating a child is not making them better. It's just going to make them worse. Like they're not going to listen to me no more.

MADISEN

Listening to Madisen. *Madisen the mouth! Boisterous, outspoken, combative, fiery and the defender of the defenseless. "No! Why can't she go to the bathroom. You just let James go. You show favoritism. He went. She should be able to go to. That's not right." She was right things weren't always right. The door slams. "That bitch get on my fuckin' nerves! If she fail me Imma smack her ass." I take a deep breath and shake my head. "Madisen! Chill out!"*

"No! I hate her!" I was relieved that no more profani-

ties spilled out this time. She pouted as she strolled to her seat. After class she came up to me to tell her story. I didn't expect an apology. The fact that she was speaking to me was enough. This was a normal exchange between Madisen and me. This was a mild disruption for Madisen. Her outbursts would set the class off and it could take twenty minutes to get them back on track. It was awful.

The Future Educator's Association at Southside went on a trip to Atlanta. Before our trip we met with the girls of Western High School, a very prestigious all girls high school in Baltimore City. We were going to be traveling on the same bus. We walked up and our group was quiet and watchful. I could see that they were intimidated. But they weren't going to show it. They observed and remained pensive. At the lunch table Madisen asked, "Aren't these olives?"

"Yes they are," I gave her a proud smile. She smirked, rolled her eyes and said "I know how to talk."

I thought that having a boyfriend was the greatest thing in the world. That was in the ninth grade. I looked school. You know, stayed out all hours of the night. Result was getting punished. And I almost failed and just all around just looking dumb. Now I look back at it like why did I do that? That was so stupid. Like, shouldn't no boy come before your education or how you feel about yourself. You shouldn't have to look towards no boy telling you you're the cutest. You should believe it yourself. I already know I'm pretty, so nobody got to tell me I'm pretty.

I just like to hear that I'm beautiful. Even though I know it, it always feels good for it to come from somebody else's mouth. I don't know, it just feels good. Like I won't say, oh he called me beautiful, I'm going to give him my jewels. No. No, thank you for the insight, thank you. That was touching. But sometimes it do irk me when he keeps saying it over and over. Okay, one time okay. You don't got to keep saying it over and over. Cause you think you're going to get a surprise and no, it don't go like that.

My first serious relationship affected me tremendously, right. I stopped liking boys - I hated boys because I thought I was in love. He loved me, told me he never wanted to cheat on me, but the devil on my back. One morning I just said something's not right. So I found out he was cheating on me. Caught him cheating- but you're the same person who said you loved me, I'm the only one, right, and yet you cheated on me. And now I look at boys like, all boys cheat, all boys liars. But that's not true because I could mess up the next chance for me for a boy that really wanted to be with me.

My father cheated on his wife and got a girl pregnant. What's that supposed to tell me? How am I supposed to feel now about boys?

Marriage is a waste of yourself because when you get married, what's yours is his and what's his is yours. So, if you get a divorce, you make more money than him, you're going to have to pay him. And if he keeps the kids, you're going to have to pay child support, so what's the point? Again, marry me? No, just stay together for a long time. You all can claim the title of being married but you don't have to necessarily **get** married.

You can't tell a teenager that condoms pop. I think like you can't tell them nothing. People tell me oh you shouldn't have sex. I don't care. I watch TV about people catching the AIDS but I still feel as though, all right, I'm having sex, I trust him. We trust each other, but it's nothing anybody can say or do that's going to stop me from doing what I do because that's just how I want to be.

6

CAREERS AND THE FUTURE

I got this all figured out now. The only way we're going to get out of here is sports. That's the only way we can get out of here. If you ain't got no talent, you ain't going nowhere. And if you got no bling, you ain't going nowhere.
MALCOLM

Baltimore is home. I feel as though when people go out of town, try to live out of town, be from a different place, you just don't fit. **DELORIS**

I think the world is coming to an end. I think that it's going to end before I get older for some reason. I just have a feeling that I'm not going to be able to live out my life because of the things that are going on in the world. I think that I'll be so stressed that I'll be in a coma and it's like I just won't wake up.
ASHLEY

DARIOUS

After high school, I'm trying to go to a school for business and engineering. Probably Morgan or Coppin or Frostburg or something. I'm trying to get my grades up. My report card is looking pretty good this quarter: Two 90's, an 80 and a 70. Once I got put out of Southside, I just got wiser and settled down. I know I got to get myself together because I know I want to be something in life and not being in life without no diploma or not even thinking about going to college. That's what I think. I mean, it is just me personally trying to learn more.

I went to the college fair yesterday, I didn't even see Coppin [State University] down there. I'm probably like West Virginia. I looked into that too. But I know I want to go for technology, engineering or somewhere in that realm.

MALCOLM

I got this all figured out now. The only way we're going to get out of here is sports. That's the only way we can get out of here. If you ain't got no talent, you ain't going nowhere. And if you got no bling, you ain't going nowhere.

Four years from now, every sport that can be played, I'm playing. If I don't get a scholarship, I'm just going to keep working. I work at Marley's Station at Journeys and I work at the flea market on the weekends.

ASHLEY

I think you should learn independence when you're a

teenager. I think it's better for every teenager to learn independence, to be independent, but then it could be a negative way. It could be a negative way because if you're too much independent, you go out thinking you can do whatever you want to do. So you can smoke and, you know, "I'm so independent I can do this all by myself." You can try to buy an apartment and all and you don't have no money to pay for the bill. No job. And you had this little bit of money. You know, teenagers like us, we feel as though if we have a couple of hundred, we got money! Three hundred dollars - that's a lot of money to me. Three hundred dollars ain't nothing! How am I going to pay the rent? How am I going to get food?

I think about teenagers getting pregnant, peer pressure, children selling drugs, babies having babies. I think about that all the time. I think things are getting worse. I think the world is coming to an end. I think that it's going to end before I get older for some reason. I just have a feeling that I'm not going to be able to live out my life because of the things that are going on in the world. I think that I'll be so stressed that I'll be in a coma and it's like I just won't wake up. That's how I feel. I just think that I'm so scared to go. The scariest thing is just closing your ears and shutting your eyes, knowing that you're not going to get back up. The scariest thing for me is sleeping, wanting to wake up so bad, but I can't get up. It can be scary for me to be in a place unknown. Being in a place and not knowing where you're at.

I just think I can be in a place so trapped and not know nobody. Nobody wants to get to know you. Everybody has their own life, their own careers. And you're just sitting there, nowhere to go. Not to Aunt Betsy's house. Nowhere to go. I just be in a dream and just have regular clothes on and just sit there.

The world [coming to] the end has something to do with

me being in a place that I don't know. It has some connection. I think about it all the time. That's why I fear it because it has something to do with the connection.

Then when I die I end up in a place that I don't even know nobody. I think that life goes on after I die. I think you just keep reliving it. I think you keep reliving on this earth. I think people who die, somebody in this earth has a part of them. They have their soul. Think about it. You have the moments when somebody comes to you and talks to you and he reminds you of this person. Or I'll be like, that person looks so familiar, but I can't recognize them. But it's not the person that you're thinking about. It's the way they do certain things. You know, the way they might wipe their eyes or they just might look familiar to you.

I feel as though that if I die I'm just going to keep shaking on my life, just trying to wake up, just wake up, wake up, and it's just never going to happen. I'm just going to get tired of doing it and then I'm just going to relive it all over and over and over again. And I hate that word "over and over again." I hate that word.

I just want it to end. Not the world to end, but I want the cycle of us doing this all over again. I want people to just think in their minds that you can be a young lady without showing off your body. I want people to know that you can be sexy but classy. You don't have to take your clothes off to get noticed. I want people to know that you are special. You are special, no matter what. No matter what this person might say. It might be like everybody might seem like they get you, but you have to keep that state of mind. You know that you're special.

I want people to know that you don't have to sit there and be like the girls in the videos because that's what I think the music wants us to do. I think the producers, the whole music biz, they want us to feel as though we have low self-esteem so we can keep buying albums to make us feel better about ourselves. And that's a good thing because you want to feel better, but I think it just portrays all into trying to be something that you're not. I think they want us to feel low self-esteem with this girl in the video, you know, "she doesn't have no clothes on, so I don't look good with no clothes on, so why don't I do this to look better?"

You know, you can't be something that you're not. You cannot do that. Then you can't even accept who you are, who you change into. Then you want to change back and you realize now you're this person so you can't change back. And you just go into your whole state of mind – what am I? I had that time when I just felt what am I? It was a long time ago, like when I was thirteen. I was young and I was just like, you know, I just did not know what to do. I was yelling for little stupid things [my friends] did – "Oh, you lied to me yesterday." I would just yell at them. Then, I'd be like "What am I?" and I would just get mad and I would just start shaking for no reason. I don't know what was going on with me.

I was just so frustrated with the world and everything around me and people doing stupid stuff around me and it just felt as though, why do we do the things we do? Why do we go smoke a joint after we get out of school? Why do we cuss like a sailor? Why do we swear all the time? Why do we want to die and then be scared to die? Why do you want to die when you know you're scared to die? Why do we do things that we don't need to do? Why do we make life – why do we make breathing so hard? Why is the air so polluted – why do we make breathing so hard? Why can't we just do what we're told? Why do we have to go through these difficult limits? Why do we try to change ourselves? Why do women let grown men beat on them?

I think about all this all the time. It's always on my mind.

The only time it's not on my mind is when I'm happy, you know, when I am meditating by myself and I'm in my own little box that I try to step out every now and then. When I come to school I might not think about it because there's so much stuff going on at school. You don't have time to think. It's like your mind is polluted.

SARAI

My aunt, she told me that the best way to have a successful life is to complete school and go to college. And she said don't have no kids at a young age even though there's nothing wrong with that because you still can go to school and complete college. She said don't have no kids and be protected. And I always listen to my aunt, even though she's not successful but she raised her daughter to be so successful.

I don't plan to stay here in Baltimore City. I want to move when I get on my own. I want to move out of here because I want to explore different places. Like Arizona. I want to go to Kansas and I just want to travel all over the world. I want to go to Mexico and Jamaica and all of them places, but first I have to get out on my own. I want to be a computer technician. But people keep telling me it's hard because you got to learn all this stuff. But I really want to be that because a lot of technology is coming along and with that you'll make a lot of money, so that's what I want to be. I want to go to college. My aunt said that I can go to college free because of my mother's disability.

But right now I'm not where I want to be because I'm not in my right grade. I'm supposed to be in eleventh [grade]. I'm trying to take the test for that, too, to get in my right grade. So it's a lot of stuff that I need to do right now before I do that and I want to go to *American Idol*. I don't know if I could sing

– my boyfriend say that I do, but I don't believe him, he's just saying that.

I do want to get married, but I don't know about kids. Because they hurt. I don't want to have kids. I'll adopt.

I don't like living in Baltimore City and I'm tired of seeing the poverty. I'm tired of seeing drugs. Like I come to school, I sit on the bus stop. I see people take drugs right in front of my face like I'm a kid and they don't care. I'm just sitting there and they just do it right there in front of my face. Like they're trying to get me to do it or something. And I hate coming up Cherry Hill. I hate coming up here because there's just a lot of things that go on up here, too much. I hate even just coming out the house because when I step out the house I don't know what might happen. So that's why I'm trying to get out of here.

I'm not ready to totally be on my own yet. Well, I am. I really want to get out of the house, because with living on my own I won't have to have no rules. I won't have to live by [my parents'] rules. But, living on my own, I still have rules because I have to pay bills, so I have to do stuff. But I don't have no rules from them. They can't tell me what to do. I told them I was going to live [at home] forever just to make them mad. And [my father] was like, when you get eighteen, get out of here. And I'm like, no uh, I'm living here until I'm sixty-five. Until I die.

LAKEDA

Listening to Lakeda. *Lakeda's slim build, calm face and small frame make her seem weak. Lakeda is quiet, studious and mature. She is very mothering, in that, she would chastise her classmates for being too loud and misbehaving. They listened and most times didn't talk back. She carried* *herself like an adult and treated them with respect and they respected that.*

I would like to be a pediatrician. I'm good with kids. I love kids. I love to teach kids and help take care of them. I think one of my reasons is because - like I said, by my mother being a single parent for so long, and she had my little brother, who is ten now and I was six at the time that she had him, I was basically left to raise him, me and my mother - so I learned a lot from that and as time went on I found my interest being in dealing with kids and helped taking care of kids. From what I'm understanding, it will take eight years after high school. It may take longer, but from what I'm understanding, it takes eight years.

DELORIS

In five years I will be twenty-one. I'll be getting out of Towson University and preparing myself for law school. Being a lawyer takes a lot of discipline because you got to sit there and read all them papers and call all the cases.

I guess I'll be making some money. I want a house and a car and all that. I'll take care of my mother. She's old now, so by the time I get up there, she's going to be older. I probably do live in Baltimore, but I'm going to be traveling.

Baltimore is home. I feel as though when people go out of town, try to live out of town, be from a different place, you just don't fit. Like, I work at the airport and I just be seeing people and they were like yeah, I'm in Baltimore, but I'm yeah, you don't belong. You don't belong. I went to Massachusetts one time and I went to Boston, and everybody had this accent and they're looking at us like no, you're not from here. Like you could, even when people don't say it, you can see it on their faces because they'd be like when you talk to them, they'd be so amazed, just in a daze. It's not that I didn't fit in. You can live anywhere else just like you live here, but I don't know. This is home. This is where I know people. We connect. And then we really connect because we all came from the same place, same situations.

TYESHA

I want to get out of school and be a business owner. I want to boss people around. I don't want to be in Baltimore no more. I just want to go away to college. I don't want to be here. I'm tired of seeing the same faces.

MELISSA

I want to be a teacher. That's why I'm in the FEA [Future Educators Association, an after-school club]. I want to teach preschool to kindergarten and own my own daycare.

You've got to go to Delaware State University. My aunt wanted to go there. I got the papers from the college fair. I don't know nothing about it. I heard about it and I wanted to go there and my aunt wanted to go there.

LAJUANE

I'm doing all right now because I'm getting older whereas I can take responsibility for certain stuff in my life that I couldn't when I was younger. I'm not still taking care of my nieces because everybody got their life together. But I got more responsibilities now. It's not another person's responsibility but it's really my duty to get stuff done myself, simple stuff, like washing clothes. I was washing clothes when I was younger, when really a parent could be doing it because I got other stuff [to do]. I shouldn't even have stress.

But just minor stuff like washing clothes, trying to get jobs, taking care of what I got to do in school and buying clothes. It's not up to me to buy my own clothes, but if I want the things that I want, I got to do it for myself. And I really don't want nobody to give it to me because now, if I don't learn now, it's going to be harder for me when I do have to learn because it's just everything going to come to me and life's just going to be hard. So I'd rather prepare myself now and take care of myself to a certain extent. I can learn from it without having to be stressed out.

People ask what do I think I'm going to do when I grow up. I really don't know because I'm multi-talented. I'm good in math. I can read very good. I understand information and people don't realize that too. It's the ability to understand information that you need to process that gets you to learn what you need to learn. Because if you don't get the information, or the right information, you're stuck.

I figured stuff out basically by growing up by myself. I was influenced basically in my whole life by just going through stuff. People pull me to the side and give me advice or they talk to me about how to deal with situations, certain situations without losing it or just maintaining focus on whatever you're doing and try to put the most energy in it that you have. But basically everything you've got, put it into what you do because that way, even if you fail or something, you can at least say well, I tried my hardest and I still failed. So it's something definite I got to get with it, I got to gain more or I got to get more or get better instead of wondering if I would have did it this way, I wonder if it would have turned out different.

When I get in the house, usually I do homework or whatever I got to do that day and I go up the street with my friend Jay. With him, we just go everywhere because he drives. You can't stay in the same environment, no matter how it is. You got to move around.

I don't know where I'll move to, but I just want somewhere different. I just want to try something different. A different environment, just not the same people because if you stay around here, your whole world is going to be Baltimore. I left out of Maryland one time and when you go somewhere else and you're looking around you see everybody different. They dress different. They talk different. Their mindset different. I just want to see how different people think and the way they influence each other compared to us. Just because something is a certain way out in Baltimore don't mean in Annapolis they do it the same way. Like it might be cool out here to rob people, but if you rob somebody out there, not everybody might leave you alone and not want to be around you and stuff like that. I just want to see how different the experience is.

I'll go to college in-state somewhere because you got family and friends around if you do need help. When you make it - when you finally do what you want to do - you got the choice to be here or be somewhere else because usually whatever college you go to I realize that's most likely where you're going to live because that's where job openings and connections and stuff happen. Like if you're going to school in Virginia. I know opportunities basically happen where you're at because if you go to school in one state, they're not going to send you to another state to train and be what you want to be.

Every college is different in teaching methods. That's why they offer different stuff, because of their surroundings. And people think it's just because of the majors in the school. It's not the majors, it's the teaching in the program itself. The program based on everything around it. Like Johns Hopkins – I live over there by Johns Hopkins on University, 33rd Street and Greenmount. When you go up there it's different – it don't even look like Baltimore. When you look around downtown, they think downtown that's it. That's the only part of Baltimore that you see, buildings. Over there [where I live], a lot of people just walking around. It's a lot students – that's just one big campus right there. Everything around it basically influences Johns Hopkins. Because if you go to Johns Hopkins and you want to go out to eat, you go out to eat and if there's people in there that's fussing and fighting and stuff, it's going to rub off on you. So, basically your surroundings mold you to be what you're going to be.

HEATH

I'd like to do physics in college, quantum mechanics, marine biology, stuff like that. I like the sciences. You know, I'm not too good at math, but I like the sciences. The math gives the science a back end, a support. A backbone. With the physics and quantum mechanics and stuff, I want to work in the theoretical section. Maybe go somewhere up in Canada over near Bar Harbor in Maine.

MIGUEL

I got my job through my uncle. He used to be the store manager at a McDonald's and the owner really liked my uncle. So once I filled out my application, I had my interview right there. He just came out and just gave me an interview and about a month later or a couple weeks later he called and asked if I was still interested in the job. I was like glad that he knew [my uncle].

The government could do something about the [legal employment] age because there's a lot of fifteen-year-olds out there and fourteen-year-olds ready to work and trying to get some money because without money, it's like you're leading yourself right into trying to get money. And the only way you're going to get money is to sell drugs. That's the only way you're going to get some money fast because you have to wait. If you're fourteen, you have to wait two, three years just to get a job and then even when you turn sixteen, you still got to wait.

They can also do something with our driver's license. I know we're teenagers and all that. They highered the standards for us and it makes it like if I go to driver's school now, I wouldn't be getting my license until 2010, 2009, you know.

It's because of how many accidents teenagers get into and all the drunk driving and it's like other teenagers make it bad for teenagers who do know how to drive and who do want it. Because coming home from work on the bus - it's just not working [for me]. I get off at 10:00 [p.m.] and don't get home until about 11:00, 11:15.

Mainly I need money for clothes. You know, we're getting bigger and bigger, clothes are getting expensive and expensive, and we got to at least help our parents out too, you know.

MCINTOSH

I don't have a job. But if I did, it would help out my mother a lot. I'm not an only child. I've got two brothers and a sister. And it's just my mother to take care of us, so it's hard on her. I've been trying to get a job and they've been kind of giving me the runaround a couple places, but I'm a good kid. I could give applications and people don't call me back. And like the time - it was the beginning of this year – they said there was supposed to be a job fair down at St. Francis. Got on a bus, went all the way over to St. Francis over east, and come to find out, no place there was hiring people that were still sixteen or seventeen. They look for like eighteen-year-olds out of high school. So that was like a long, long bus ride over there. No place was looking. Well, there was one place. It was a hospital, but the hours wasn't going to work because I still go to school.

TARENA

Listening to Tarena. *Tarena lives with her grandparents. Her parents are around but she doesn't have a solid relationship with them. She is friendly, outgoing, popular and loud. Her grandparents keep her in check and in school everyday. Now class is another story. Tarena is not a frequent class hooker but at times can easily get caught up with the crowd. Her tenth grade year proved to be a rebellious year. The calm and smiling Tarena escaped over the summer. Most times she can easily be coaxed back.*

Well, I don't have no job right now, but I will have a job this summer. I went to Youth Works Monday to take my application in. Everything is going okay. And by the end of this summer, I will have a job, a part-time job and I'll be okay.

What I want to be is a pediatrician or a nurse. And if I feel as though that doesn't work out, I will go to the Army Reserves. But it's going to work because I'm going to make it work. It's times that I just feel like I don't want to do this, but it's going to get better. Once I get to college – I've got two more years of high school, so fine. By my twelfth grade year I'll have my mind set what I want to do.

My dream is to be successful, to be more successful than my parents were, try to be better than my parents were.

Why do the world have to come to an end? Why can't it just keep going? Like the last time the world came to an end by water. This time it's going to be by fire. I want to know why does it have to end. Why it can't just keep going and going for many and many years?

7

POLITICS AND SOCIETY

Obama! To have a black president - it make me feel good. The word of the year is "Yes We Can." We can do anything because we came from nothing to something. We made our first and more to come for our black presidents.
DARIOUS

I think Barack Obama will make changes to the school, maybe. Like helping out in the schools with supplies and all that. **ISAIAH**

Things don't change overnight and you can't expect one person to help things change. If you want something to change just as well as they want something to change, you can put your thoughts and ideas together and you can have something. **LAKEDA**

DEINERA

The city[government] of Baltimore should have more determination. I don't know all of them, but based on the way everything going, they're not pushing things the way they should. Like, I said, the teachers ain't pushing the kids to do right. The police ain't pushing to get stuff right. That's just my own thing. I feel like they're not determined and they doing what they have to do to not get complaints. But they're not doing all that they can do to make things right.

AARON C.

I think that the government could make our lives here in Cherry Hill better if they lowered all the tax rates. They should lower it because a lot of parents out here is single parents taking care of these kids. I mean, I ain't speaking only on behalf of me – my brother and some classmates from out of school that I know of and everybody I know whose mother is raising them by themselves. Their father is nowhere around. With high taxes, they have less money to take care of their household.

I ain't going to say they should put more [surveillance] cameras up, but [the police] should ride through a lot to keep people off the corners and stuff like that. People got little cousins, little sisters and little babies out here in this world and you don't want to bring them up around that environment.

I was told that the [surveillance cameras] ain't work, but I don't believe it. I don't think they just put the camera up if it don't work. I think it helps because it might be somebody who was about to do a shooting or something out here, he'll look up and "Oh man, there's a camera right there. No, I ain't doing that. I'll just do it later or something like that." I think that scares people because they know they're being watched.

DELORIS

Listening to Deloris. *"Pitbull in a skirt" is how the rapper Eve refers to herself. However, this analogy is more fitting for Deloris. She is a tiny girl and looks way too young to be in high school. She is a junior and has yet to develop a great affinity for boys. Books, knowledge, and debate are her preference. She was a member of the Future Educator's Association, the debate team, the step team, Students Helping Other People, and a few others.*

As a debate team member, she was a fierce competitor and even before the debate team was formed she displayed her prowess for debate in class. She was a part of a class that included Deinera, Janae, Gage, Darious, Choc and other strong-willed individuals. She agreed and disagreed forcefully and respectfully. She made sure you understood her point.

This class by far was the class that challenged me the most. They challenged me to provide more rigor, to listen to them, their opinions and ideas and at times change my own. She and Janae gave a PowerPoint presentation on telekenesis and telepathy. The class was intrigued and in awe. They asked questions and she stood confident and answered all their questions without hesitation. She had done her research.

On the surface she seems to have it together. However, as I got to know Deloris, I understood why she was so driven. Her home life wasn't the best and she was determined to make her life better and to make it count. If I ever need legal representation I would definitely utilize her services.

American society is terrible because the rich get rich, the poor get poorer. Even though we try to fix the system, everybody becomes corrupt. It's just terrible.

I see no hope [in politicians]. Most people who do get in office become corrupt by all of the pressure and the temptations of doing favors for somebody and somebody else doing favors for you and you making this person happy and sacrifice certain things for the citizens. No.

There's no hope. And then the war - we just don't know what to do about that because I thought the war was over and then it's still going on. And it's still going on and we can't bring the troops home. We just can't leave Iraq the way it is. If we leave to bring the troops home, look at Iraq. Iraq's just going to be just the way it is and the war that was fought over there is going to be fought on our territory. And not only that, it's going to be wrong for us to go over there and uproot their leader, cause a whole bunch of chaos and then just leave.

The way you live your life is affected by society. People can make change somewhat, but not drastically. Like, say Barak Obama gets in office. I think he is the definite candidate that actually will cause the most drastic changes in the United States. So if he gets in office, there is going to be some type of changes, but then again, it's too much behind, like what's going on right now, to actually change it.

We have a problem right now - poverty is our problem. You can probably solve the problem of poverty for right now, but you've got to go behind it. Like why are people becoming poor, how rapidly are they becoming poor? You can't do that with the whole United States.

Hillary Clinton can make changes and I think she definitely will, like with healthcare and all that, but not to the point, or not drastically enough where Barak Obama can. If both of them was in office right now, I think he would do the most, or if not the most, if Hillary Clinton does more, his would be more effective though. She has too much political history behind her. And I know for a fact that the first thing she's going to deal with when she's in office is healthcare or whatever. But she tried to solve that problem already and they convinced her and paid her off and she shut right up. You know what I'm saying? She's got too much political history, owes too many people favors, behind politics and all that.

Why is everything the way it is? Like why am I here? Why is society like this? How can it change? And would it be different if something else were to take place? Like Africa. Let's take Africa for example. Why was Africa so powerful at one point in time when they took Greeks and Romans and had gold and all that? If Europe didn't come down and try to take over and all that, what differently would have been happening? Would Africa have been the top continent instead of North America? And even though it did happen, how can you change it? Africa's in poverty, has a bunch of AIDS now. How can you change that?

And then like today you see how we have videos and all that stuff, would Africa be like that and we'd be the poor continent? We're considered western technology and then it's considered eastern savage, so would it be eastern technology versus western savage? I don't know. I just wonder. A big old accident of history. And then too much power made some things like the Mongolian Empire tried to take over the Somali Empire and then all of it crashed and that's what made them vulnerable.

Some of the things that happen now in the United States, I feel as though if we had somebody to protect us against it, we could stop it. Like Bush - why would you create the Patriot Act? You can just detain people, have no warrants, no search and seizure, don't tell them anything. Well, that's an abuse of power. I don't even understand why that was passed because it's unconstitutional. I think they just passed it to pass it because that was thick. That's 3,000-something pages that each congressman's got to read and it was passed in less than four days.

We tried to go over there and take over Iraq when George Senior was in office. We was cool with Saddam Hussein – yeah, his name is Saddam Hussein. Because we gave that man too much power and - I think that's what happened - the United States was too much in supreme. We were going over there and telling you do this, you do this and I guess people felt enriched because they had some delegated power. That was just a big collision. And honestly, I think if all those countries that did not like the United States all came together, we would be wiped out. Because look how much Iraq did to us. Look how much we're going through with Iraq. We spend billions of dollars on that war a day.

We are in the hole economically. I don't even recall the United States having a budget surplus. And I feel as though every president that gets in office wants to declare war, like it is a presidential duty to declare war. Why? Even when George Washington was in office we had a war. Every president wants to declare war.

And then they throw words out like terrorism, freedom. They're words, people, words! Think about it now. You are being terrorized. You don't have any freedom for real. And I don't even understand why they keep people – I guess it's just something people don't know. And that's because they don't teach you in school. And this is another reason I want to be a criminal defense attorney. The government can tell you what to put in the schools. In school, they don't tell us everything we're supposed to know. They don't tell us about post-colonial movements and the stuff I said about Africa. You've gotta look that stuff up on your own. They tell us stuff like the United States government is run like this, this and this. The president is good, good, but they don't tell us stuff like you can advocate against them and stuff like that. You gotta learn that type of stuff on your own.

I learn from people telling me and you have to have common sense. This is another reason why I think I have ADHD. Because ADHD people look at things differently. Like when I said that about Africa, it used to be I didn't even look at that like that. You know what I'm saying? I didn't look at it like that – I just looked at it differently. Like, if I read the paper and it say that George Bush is going over to Iraq to solve the country, I look at it as him going over there and imperializing them people even more. How are you going to force democracy on somebody? That's not democracy if you're forcing it on somebody. That's more like communism being called democracy under control or something.

And then even if they did [force democracy on Iraq], who's going to be the leader? How's the country going to be ran? It took the United States a long time for us to do that. And then we had several documents, too, like the Magna Carta, we had a whole bunch of documents before we came up with the Constitution. And it's like schemes inside the United States government. Why are you trying to find loopholes on what the president can and cannot do just because it's not directly stated? That's what I think.

AARON S.

The war in Iraq is stupid pretty much. It's stupid. It's all about money. We ain't need it. Ain't nobody coming in our houses blowing our head off, not like that over here. Why should we go over there and do it? They people is like we people.

I think it will be over soon as we get a new president. Barack, all day. Barack, all day. It's going to be a change when Barack come. Everybody going to lighten up. It's going to be a lot of pressure off us black men, I would say. I wouldn't just say black people period, it's going to be a lot of pressure off black men. Because at the end of the day we're going to be in charge now. It's just different. It's going to be a lot different. I just can't wait.

He already did change people's opinion of black men, just by running for president. He did it right there. Just to show people that we can do it. Right there. That changes it right there. You see how people can change already. So imagine once he gets into office or if he do not get in office, people will still love Barack. Just for what he did.

Day after the election, I might just, I ain't going to say go off. Yeah, I might just go out and treat myself to something to eat, just be happy to be black. Because black people came a long way now, I guess. A long way. You couldn't see no black man running for no president 1865. He would have got his head cut off or something like that, for even having a conversation about running for president. So for Barack to have enough nuts or balls if you want to say to even run for it - he a man. Yeah, he ain't worried about his family getting assassinated. I won't say he's not worried, but he put his people before anything. He put his people before anything.

There's definitely a fear that he could be assassinated because - with the white man - he ain't having it. There ain't been no black [president] - he going to be the first. Never been in there. He going to be the first, so there ain't been none before. So, why would they stop it now? Why would they, why would they just let a black man get in office in 2008?

That's a definite fear for black men. They cut his whole family up and don't nobody know. They didn't do anything. They run everything, the Congress, everything. They could just assassinate his whole family, everybody last name Obama, or Barack, anything. They could just kill them. And then just make up a lie, say he had a car accident. They could frame those and get away with it. It's because they run everything. So just to give a black man the power to say I'm in charge, I make decisions and no more war in Iraq. We ain't getting no more money off oil. I'm going to give out more jobs, more money to teachers. And a black man said that? They take his head off quick.

CHOC

Listening to Choc. *Choc's smiling face is a beautiful thing. His head is covered with thick long dreadlocks and his face is dark. His gold fronts cover his front top teeth. He looks rough and tough but he is a sweetie. He is full of compliments and inspirational words. He always responded with "Yes ma'am" and "Sir." He was a very respectful young man. I knew Choc smoked marijuana so I wasn't shocked when he was caught in the bathroom by Officer R--.*

The government can do a lot of things to make schools better, starting off with more money for the school, more books, you know. When you're in class you've got to share books with students and what not. So I just say, more activities for the youth, I say. More activities, more trips. Things like that. Like this youth organization. It keeps teens out of trouble, away from drugs, gangs and violence and stuff like that. I was in the program since I was like nine or ten or eleven. I got in and my brother got me in the program and I sell candy. You get paid commission, you know, whatever you put in your work, that's what you get out of it or whatever. So I sell candy. I go around, I ask people do they like to purchase stuff.

I feel as though Obama can make a change in my community. I mean, I feel as though he a great leader since he been talking and I been listening. It's a change that we need with him being a black president. It really don't matter, but I just like because he is a different opinion, he got a different view on the world so I feel as though like he's the best man for that versus McCain or whatever, the same thing repeating itself, same thing with Bush. So, it's just a change that we need. Like the war in Iraq should be over, shouldn't it? I really don't like war, so just the war itself should be stopped. I mean, what we fighting over, a little oil, I think? I feel as though the war should end for many reasons, many reasons.

HEATH

Apparently [the presidential candidates] are disagreeing about stuff, which is stupid. I don't understand why you'd be focusing on their piddly squabbling and the squabbling between Obama and Clinton and McCain, you know, just because she's having drinks with – what were they, union people in a bar and he said something about Pennsylvania people? Yeah, I'm like, why? So what? He said it.

And the media blows it up out of proportion. You should be worried about their promises, whether or not they're going to keep them, their actual goals, the plans they're setting in motion now.

I want to say I'm neither optimistic nor pessimistic about the future of this country because no matter what, it's not going to change my outlook or what I'm going towards. Who's president and why they're squabbling or what not. No matter which one is president, I'm depending on myself not anyone else. It doesn't matter if you go over here and you mess up XYZ, I'm going this way no matter what.

DARIOUS

The government don't give the citizens enough money and support. They should help out more. People out here are struggling and we got basic rights for government to help us out and I don't think they're doing their job good enough. They could be doing more.

Obama! To have a black president - it make me feel good. When I was in government class, my teacher asked me how does it make me feel. I said that it makes me feel that we can strive for the best and positive. The word of the year is "Yes We Can." We can do anything because we came from nothing to something. We made our first and more to come for our black presidents.

But some things are still going to be the same because it's going to take a lot of years. I mean, he can't just change the world in one year. It's going to take him several years to change. And maybe, after him, the next president's still going to have to make a change. But then he can just make improvements for the change.

DUANE

Barack Obama, I like how he's cool because he could probably be our first black president and I was kind of worried for him because I thought he probably be assassinated or something. You know, anybody that gets in high power like Martin Luther King and Malcolm X. As soon as they get some high power, they get assassinated.

Yeah, I think Barack Obama would be cool because he's got a lot of people rooting for him and the whites are rooting for him, too.

It's still all about the money because Obama will say he never has enough money so it ain't like what are you going to do for us because I don't really think he can do much. 'Cause it's still about the money. He can't throw a couple million to the schools because they trying to bring the troops home and that's going to cost money.

That George Bush guy really messed up. He already messed up a lot of stuff, so Barack Obama got to come in and fix it. He has to clean up George Bush's mess because George Bush made a lot of mistakes – a lot of mistakes. Especially taking the troops to Iraq, saying there was mass weapons of destruction and the reality is that he just wanted Saddam Hussein.

ISAIAH

I think Barack Obama will make changes to the school, maybe. Like helping out in the schools. Supplies and all that. And young children in school and stuff.

Then there's no weapons [in Iraq] so now what, they're using weapons that we sold to Iraq. That's crazy. They keep shooting up and bombing people.

LAKEDA

In some ways I think that Obama can change things because he's more familiar with the society and he seems like he has a lot of advice and lot of plans. But it's been a lot of other people who seem like they were familiar with this society and had a lot of plans, but once they get into office, it's like everything they say that they're going to do, all of a sudden changes.

I feel like if the society - if parents and teachers and the government, if everyone, all adults - get more involved in their kids' lives and if they can build more recreation centers instead of building more jails and giving us more activities to do so that we wouldn't always have to be in the street. It's a lot of stuff that can be built or you can spend and put effort forth into besides a jail or different things.

In the area that I live in, there's a basketball court, there's a gym, there's a recreation center and I see that a lot of kids are involved in the recreation center. It's a lot of sports, football, basketball, it's the recreation center have a lot of games. They have little kiddie discos and parties for the kids, so it's very interesting. It gives the kids something to do instead of being outside, getting into this gang, standing on this corner, selling these drugs. It gives them time to realize who they can really be in life instead of being someone that's going to be on the corner and make nothing of themselves.

Maybe things will change over time, but I think it's going to take more than politics and more than just the government. It takes everyone. You can't just rely on one person to change the world and a lot of people feel like, well, if we put him in office, this can happen. But when they say "Oh will this, that and the third can happen?" they feel like it can happen overnight. Things don't change overnight and you can't expect one person to help things change. If you want something to change just as well as they want something to change, you can put your thoughts and ideas together and you can have something.

8

RACISM AND POVERTY

In school, black children don't get as much as the white children, but that's kind of a situation that you're in control of. You got to do it yourself, you know, children got to study on their own. If you don't have a lot of textbooks, go to the library or something. Try to teach yourself if you can't get taught fully at school. And if you want to get out of this situation, then you need education to get out of it. **TORI**

I guess I was raised thinking that if you're a minority you get special privileges. Maybe the physically handicapped should get support, but when it comes to ethnicity, no, because that doesn't make you any less smarter to need the scholarship or grant. **HEATH**

I really see being a young black male is different than being a white male. But I can handle it cause I already been through it. **AARON S.**

TORI

My sister has encountered racism but no one's ever been racist to me. I've seen people – I've seen it on TV and stuff.

I mean, I won't mess up the person, try to beat them up or anything, unless they try to hurt me. When people say something to you about your race and stuff, it's like the same thing as somebody calling you a name. It's a big deal, but that's basically all they're doing, calling you nigger and stuff like that – they're just calling you names, unless they're trying to be violent with you.

In school, black children don't get as much as the white children, but that's kind of a situation that you're in control of, too. See, people complain about "Oh, we don't get this" and "They try to put us down by trying to teach us this and we don't understand it." But you got to do it yourself, you know, children got to study on their own. If you don't have a lot of textbooks, go to the library or something, you know. Try to teach yourself if you can't get taught fully at school. And if you want to get out of this situation, then you need education to get out of it. They won't do that anymore. They won't help. But it's mostly like the poor schools and mostly black children go to poor schools.

DUANE

I find - I don't know if it's true or not, it could be true or false - I feel that the people that make the most money pay the less taxes. And that's crazy. So that means the poor struggle. If you ain't got that much money, they try and keep you down. I mean, that's what they're doing.

It's all about education. Really education alone is a piece

of paper – a diploma, a bachelor's degree and anything you major in. If you've got that, you can do whatever you want to do.

DELORIS

The rich get rich, the poor get poorer. It's not 'cause you're just poor. It's rare that somebody who has no money is going to open a business. But if you have the money, you're going to open a business and raise the prices no matter how much you want to and nobody else can do anything about it because they don't have the money to support themselves. And then that's how people become poor and then they raise their children in poor places and they can't get the education they need to become in the status to open a business so it's a revolving cycle.

Say one person does get out and becomes a little richer. They're going to do different things like take Raven - she started off as an actress. She's a singer/actor/dancer, does movies, all of that now. She getting a whole bunch of money. Tyler Perry started off as a playwright at Morgan State. He got money, movies, songs. He don't even be in the movies half the time anymore. He just pays actors to do it for him. And then, on top of that, movie, let's just say a movie costs a million dollars to make, but in return, because so many people go see it, you made three million dollars. So you just profited two million dollars. The rich get richer, and the poor get poorer.

Once you have money, it just keeps coming. Not unless you just dumb and don't reinvest it in anything. If you were dumb and didn't know how to invest your money, it's because you didn't have the proper education and really it's the people that are rich are smart enough to know that they can turn that money into more money.

I don't know how people can say Obama's going to get

the black vote because he's not fully black – you know what I'm saying? That's one thing I didn't like pushed about him, you can't say you want the black vote because you're not fully black. You can't say you're something if you don't have that full potential. But, since he doesn't say I want the black vote – he wants the "change vote"– so, yeah.

Most Americans think he's black, because that's their not knowing or ignorance. Like back in the old times, if you were mixed, you were still considered black. That's just ignorant. I don't think of him as black. People that's mixed, I do not consider you black. I just don't. You're mixed. Like on a form or something to vote, you pick "other." He really can't go for the black vote if you're not fully black.

AARON S.

Somebody needs to solve our money crisis. It's not just the current [money crisis] – it's been around. There's so many homeless people in Baltimore, a lot of homeless people and just people that ain't got it right at all and can't go get it. I think there should be more jobs, more opportunities for people, so people can put food on their table. A lot of people in Baltimore got kids and stuff like that. And they just ain't got it.

There are a lot of jobs that people could do who sit around all day - just like the people that go to work every day. They make it difficult saying that you need a diploma or a degree to go clean up a gym but people clean up in the house every day. I think they shouldn't make you have a degree or a diploma for a lot of jobs, like the easy jobs where you sit at a desk all day and be on a computer half the time. People are home on the computer all the time on MySpace all day and really not working, but they can't get a job because they don't got certification or qualifications that the person want.

My mother and my father have prepared me for society's racism since day one. Ain't nobody going to come home and pay your rent. Ain't nobody, don't nobody else but you. Don't nobody put food on your table but you. So why listen to somebody or why worry about what they think if they ain't doing nothing for you? They ain't putting no money in your pocket. They ain't taking care, they ain't washing your clothes, they ain't doing nothing. So like, my father put that in my head at a young age - don't worry about nobody else. You go to school for you. You do what you got to do for you. 'Cause ain't nobody else going to do it for you.

Being black has an impact on who I am because if I was a young sixteen-year-old male, white or Caucasian, I would probably be in a better predicament than what I'm in today. I work. I drive. But I did that because of my parents. I see young sixteen-year-old males, they got Corvettes, everything. I drive a '95 Pontiac Grand Am. I go to work every day. My mother don't put no money in my pocket, nothing, nobody but me. So when I see sixteen-year-old males driving Corvettes and living in Essex or Anne Arundel County at a $900,000 house or their parents giving them an allowance - I ain't never seen an allowance a day in my life. We ain't know about that in my house at all.

So I really see being a young black male is different than being a white male. But I can handle it cause I already been through it. If I'm still on the same track, I'm going to mature and mature and mature and become a man and I already know the struggle, I've already been through it, so when I do get successful and I do get my $900,000 house or my Corvette, I ain't going to be stupid with it because I already been through my '95 Grand Am and not seeing an allowance and going to work for myself and everything. That would keep me settled and not acting crazy.

ISAIAH

Racial for me, I ain't got a problem. I can get along with other people, you feel me? I don't got a problem with nothing. As long as you don't got a problem with me.

I had a problem with a bunch of white hillbillies. They was driving one day, me and my cousin was walking up the street. And they was crossing over, so they told us to "Get the f-- off the street, niggers." So then my cousin was like, "Man, why don't you get out?" So then, they turn and they get out. They had swords and chains and stuff. So then we get to take off running.

HEATH

I define myself as Caucasian, white, whatever you want to call me. I don't like ethnicity anyway in anyone. The label. Everyone is trying to label everyone these days with racial ethnicity, religion, and I just think it holds people back anyway. Like when they give the kids the forms to fill out for college courses they would have to take. At the bottom it's like you're accepted for a grant if you're this racial ethnicity and I'm like, that's stupid.

And then, of course, if you're a minority and stuff, but I think just as a label, it holds people back. You know, he's black, he's Asian. Asian people are smart but bad drivers. I just think it holds everyone back and we should just get rid of it altogether.

[Caucasians are stereotyped as] hillbilly, honkies who

drive buggies and wear straw hats. You know, I'm smart. Therefore, they think because I'm white, everyone in the school that's white is smart. My friend Eric's white and he's just real dumb. So, yeah, I think [the black students] are racist when it comes to a degree, not in a bad way. Some of my friends aren't. But, yeah, I think they have some stereotypes going on at school. It doesn't hold me back - why would it? It's obviously not true. I wouldn't believe it, so it's not going to hold me back.

I guess I was raised thinking that that if you're a minority you get special privileges. Maybe the physically handicapped should get support, but when it comes to ethnicity, no, because that doesn't make you any less smarter to need the scholarship or grant. I can understand financially-wise, but ethnicity has nothing to do with it.

If people would just believe in themselves and try to go for what they need, what they want and achieve their goals, you know, then they won't be poor. They're just, you know, that's where they – I don't want to say *want* to be - but that's where they've been placed and they're afraid to get out of that so they're just going to live there in that level because they don't think they can go up, but they can.

I don't think [Obama and Clinton] should be labeled as the first black president or the first female president. I think they should just be – you should be looking towards what they're talking about. What their goals are. What they're trying to achieve in the presidency instead of being labeled as the first black president which everyone in the school is talking about. I hate it because they keep saying it's going to be reverse slavery. And I'm like, if it's reverse slavery, it means the slaves are going to own the slave master. I'm like, that doesn't make sense. So you mean it shouldn't be called slavery.

And it wouldn't happen now. I mean, I'm not in Congress or anything, but there's black senators and governors and mayors, you know. So why wouldn't there be a black president? But I don't think they should just be labeled as the first black president or the first female president.

And they shouldn't give privileges to certain people. And if they do, they should be impeached right away. They shouldn't be allowed to do that, depending on any ethnicity or whatever gender. But, in the presidency I don't like it because they just squabble over what each other says.

MALCOLM

If [Obama] is president, the world is coming to an end. Because the people that still racist going to be mad. They're going to start tearing down stuff because it's a black president. And if the woman wins, the men are going to have a problem with it because they're going to say it's the man's world. Man's world. It is a problem that if Hillary Clinton do be president, the men ain't going to like it. Other men ain't going to like that 'cause they're greedy.

I learned to respect women because I had no father and I had to do everything myself. When your mother takes care of you, you come out different. When you just got a mother, you see what they go through. That's how you're going to be.

AARON C.

Listening to Aaron C. *Aaron C. could be the happiest kid I know. He is always smiling and always friendly. Mischievous at the least but still a great kid. I never taught Aaron but seeing him in the hall hooking a class or on his way to the office because he was put out of class, I got to* *know him pretty well. I also taught his brother Darious. He is playful and kind.*

If I could change my life, I wouldn't be here in Baltimore. But I'll get my education and get up out of here. It's hard out here for us, for all black African-Americans. I mean, I heard they're requiring a high school diploma just to get a job at McDonald's now. It's getting real hard for us black teenagers out here and I just think everybody needs to stay focused.

Racism is still going on in some parts of the world. I just don't like the fact that anybody had us African Americans as slaves. Like when they told us to do something, they beat us and I just – I'm all against that. I don't like that. And it made me at first not like white people, but after a while I realized it wasn't that white person in particular who beat my people, it might have been one of his family members or his ancestors that beat our peoples. And I was told, I don't know how true it is, I was told that the only reason why people that are light-skinned or light brown, I was told that the white man raped our ancestors. That's what I was told. I don't know how true it is though.

SARAI

Living in Baltimore, you're going to get discouraged a lot because there's a lot of things in the world that just try to stop you, especially being black, too. It's a lot of things trying to stop you, especially being black. People don't want you to succeed.

I think sometimes the Caucasians get the better service and better things than we do. Like you go in a county school where a lot of Caucasians are at, they got better desks, better books, newer stuff, and you come to our school and our desks are raggedy and stuff and they say it's because we don't want to learn anything. But I think it is not because we don't want to learn anything, it's because they mistreated us so long that we don't really know what to do when we finally got the stuff, when we finally got books, when we finally got to be not segregated. So, that's what I think. So it's like the Caucasians get the better service than we do. And I think even Mexicans get better service than we do.

Sometimes I think it's racism that happens. Like, when I was younger, I was in the fifth grade and if I blamed something on a Caucasian, then I would really get in trouble for it. The principal would be like, yeah, you did it. If she blamed something on me, I did it, but if I blamed something on her, she didn't really get it as bad as I got it from the principal [who was Caucasian]. So it's a lot of difference. It's still a lot of differences between us and I really think that if Obama wins, I'm not saying that I want him to win – I don't know who's going to win – but I'm not saying that Hillary Clinton's not like that either. I'm just saying that if Obama won, then maybe they'll look into it and see how blacks are getting mistreated and stuff still today.

I think it's black peoples' job to help themselves, but I don't know. I just don't know. They need more people to influence them. A lot of new leaders. I think they need a lot of leaders, role models and stuff.

Poems by Ashley

Why do you stereotype?
Black males with guns
And why do you walk around harassing everyone?
Is it just us? Why not them?
Strong men with guns, a shiny silver badge
Gives you the right to harass
The right to judge
The right to push and shove
While we stand still
A voice not to be heard
In a crowd full of flowers
Blue uniforms and birds
You don't care so we fear
The need not to be scared
Just like everyone
So we don't run
Don't fight with our fists
But the power of words
Will unleash our fear
To stand tall and take a chance
And now
We R men

I Know a Queen
I know of a lady great and tall loves to teach
poetry, English and all
A wonderful lady
Black and a queen
Smile like the sun
Eyes as pretty as a dream
She is a Black woman
A queen of love
Although her throne hasn't arisen
Her crown is above
Although she looks peaceful
Pain in her eyes
Above it all she survives
She survives the pain and the hurt
Of what people say
She is a strong Black woman
With bravery painted on her face.

9

CRIME AND VIOLENCE

I never really hung with the wrong people. I don't really hang outside, there ain't too much to do out Cherry Hill. Every day - not every day – somebody getting hurt. **AARON C.**

The more police you've got around to harass, the more people are going to come out to act out. And it will keep going. And I don't really think [Sheila Dixon], George Bush, any political person want drugs to stop. It employs too many people. Judges, bail bondsmen, lawyers. **DUANE**

I was going to write to the mayor because I didn't understand - why are things like they are in Baltimore City? And I was just thinking like if I live somewhere else, would it be different? **SARAII**

LAJUANE

A lot of people do crimes because they wonder how stuff will work if they had or if they get something like that. Like, robbery. I know people that have robbed somebody before or something and I asked them - I wouldn't ask them the way I'm telling you because we're in a different environment – but basically explain. And I asked them why did you do it? What was the purpose? Because most of the time it don't even be for what you get. You'll get money, but when you're robbing somebody, you don't know what they have in their pockets. You don't know if they have money or not. You're just wondering if they got money in their pocket, if it's a possibility, the way they look. If they look like they don't got money, you're not going to rob 'em. I can't say it's fun for them, but it's the mindset growing up in that situation that in order to get something they think they've got to take it because even if they work, they still might not get it.

And people don't realize that when they say good things come to people that wait, that's not necessarily true because you can wait and stuff can just not go your way. And by being human, you want things that you like and by us being in poverty a lot, and growing up around here, we see a lot of stuff that we want and never have. So when you get the opportunity to get it, you try to get it in any kind of way. If you ask somebody out here, they'll probably tell you "because I wanted it." They don't ever think of the consequences or how the other person got it, that they're getting it from. How do they know I can rob you and as soon as I rob you, somebody can rob me not knowing it wasn't even mine from the beginning? I got it from you. And I say if you do it to somebody else, what makes you think somebody else worse than you will not do it to you?

AARON C.

I never really hung with the wrong people. I don't really hang outside, there ain't too much to do out Cherry Hill. Every day - not every day - somebody getting hurt. I ain't going to say getting shot. Every day somebody getting hurt out here. I mean, I just want to keep my head up. I'll be out here and my little brother will be out here. I don't want to have him in the streets by himself.

I just wonder why we live in the same hood and we all are beefin' with each other. Like, you go over east or west or even Westport and all of them stick together. But we're out here in the small community in Cherry Hill projects and everybody want to take everybody sides. You might have the Up The Hill boys beefin' with Down The Hill boys and Coppin Court beefin' with some boys, but all of us are living in Cherry Hill. It's so close to where you lay your head. They just need to stop. Somebody going to end up getting hurt. Somebody family member. I lost my little cousin to violence a good two, three years ago named Lil Stink. I wish grown men who know they got power or not even that, just a motivational speaker to come and take everybody together and be all right. You all need to just squash it and just stop the violence and whatever out here. And if you can't find no way by yourself, go to church - the Lord will change your life.

DARIOUS

I think that Cherry Hill is one of the worst places in Baltimore. You got drugs getting sold. You can't even sit on your porch without you thinking somebody's going to shoot at you for no reason. People walk through that's not from around the way and then you see somebody else who they beefin' with – they going to bang at you and then both of y'all are going to get caught up in a situation you ain't even belong in. Like once a month or every three months you're going to hear about somebody getting shot or killed out Cherry Hill. I guess the average three months in between that time. Or the police harass somebody. Just a lot of stuff going on.

What would make things better for teenagers in Cherry Hill is if they would give more programs for people to go to and just give back to the needy. They don't really got no shopping centers or stores up there. They could hook us up with a nice market to go to, more police or less killing, and trouble wouldn't go on. Or police that do their job, not just harass innocent people. It has happened to me more than five times. Just walking past and the police think I'm selling drugs or doing something violent. They just drive past and they jump all over us for no reason. Throw us on the ground. Search us for no reason. We just sitting somewhere and they just run up on us with their guns out, walking around and they just stop and pull their car in front of us, jump out for no reason. Instead of getting people they know innocent, they can be out there finding criminals. I'm pretty sure they have a clue who the criminals are. I mean, it been a lot of people got locked up, who suffering in jail. Or, if they don't [know the criminals], they know the areas where they can go at.

There is not really gangs in Cherry Hill. It's like neighborhood things. You from one way. You from up the hill. You from hillside. You from Coppin Court. And they all beefin' against each other. I mean, you can call it a gang, but it's not like the Bloods and Crips. It's not as big as the Bloods and Crips or like any other gang like that. It's just like my block doesn't like your block. And that been going on for years.

Even when my father and them was going through this, they still is like separating and going through a lot of trials and tribulations.

AARON S.

A lot of people, they get killed in Baltimore, young people my age, around my age or a little bit older. A lot of my home boys get killed, get shot. So everywhere I go I just take precautions like I make sure I'm safe basically. I make sure ain't nothing about to happen to me. When I'm outside I might be with three or four of my home boys and nine times out of ten, two of them got guns.

DUANE and ISAIAH

Listening to Duane and Isaiah. *Duane and Isaiah both came to Southside from a juvenile detention center. Each quiet, Isaiah more than Duane, reserved and mature for ninth graders. Duane came during the second week of school and was eager to share and succeed. He reasoned that jail was not the place for him. He did well. He participated, completed assignments and then his attendance began to slip. "It's money out there Ms. Stone. I gotta get that dough cheese (money). Don't nobody help me. I got somewhere to live but that's about it. My peoples don't take care of me." I felt for him. I had been teaching for nine years and had seen it all too often. He admitted that it was not a job that he wanted for the rest of his life but, "I gotta do what I gotta do."*

Then Isaiah came to school. He was a thin boy with cornrows and gold fronts. He came to school towards the end of our first unit and excelled as if he had been there the entire time. Their short stories were due in three days. I gave him verbal instructions and one opportunity at revising and he mastered in a twenty-minute discussion what had taken the rest of the class an entire quarter. He incorporated masterfully the elements of a story and imagery. His story was suspenseful, exciting and creative. It was the story of his arrest.

What I didn't realize was that Isaiah and Duane were friends. Very soon after Isaiah began to excel, he began to have his own attendance issue. Nevertheless, he was a much more frequent visitor than Duane. I often sent messages to Duane about coming to school and Isaiah relayed them. Many times they worked. "I told him Ms. Stone. He said he was coming today." These guys were true friends but they had their own issues to deal with. Often they would encourage each other. They made deals with each other that they would both come to school. I would see them in the hall together and give them a stern talking to. "Yo? What did we just talk about yo?" Duane would ask Isaiah. "We said we gon' come to school everyday." Then Isaiah assured me that the only reason he came to school was to come to my class. I was flattered but, "my class is not the only class you need to graduate."

"Alright Ms. Stone."

Duane: I want to talk about the mayor, what's her name? Sheila Dixon. I don't even know what she thinks she's doing to clean up the city for real because there's not really much that she could do for real. But she sends more police out there to do more harassing and that ain't getting nowhere because more people are going to act out. The more police you've got around to harass, the more people are going to come out to act out. And it will keep going. And I don't really think her, George Bush, any political person want drugs to stop. It employs too many people. Judges, bail bondsmen, lawyers –

Isaiah: In Baltimore City, what else is there to really talk about but murders and drugs? Murders and drugs. That's why there's a lot of police. For murders and drugs.

The police are dirty. Police take people's money when they stop you. They see you got money, they're going to take it. Like my man, for instance. We was out one day walking. We was coming from basketball practice. So then the police pulled us over. It was like yeah, we sawed you somewhere in the alley. We said we was just coming from basketball. We had our shorts and our ball and shoes and stuff. Then they put my man to the side like that. So, then they are talking to him and the next thing I know they're putting the cuffs on him. Yeah, they're putting the cuffs on him. And I was hey yo, what's going on? And he was like they're putting something on me. And I'm like, shit, it ain't right.

Duane: And then sometimes they use people, police departments use people as quotas. Even though I know it's what they gotta do, but still it's like they got to have a certain amount of people locked up by the end of the month. You shouldn't do it like that. You gotta have quotas – that means that if nobody don't do nothing wrong, you still gotta lock somebody up. It's like a business. People depend on people getting locked up. People definitely depend on crime. Like judges, they wake up, new cases every day. They see new faces every day. Probably the same old faces they're sick and tired of.

Isaiah: My man came home the next day. Spent the night in booking. He had to go to court, though. They gave him probation. Juvenile probation. They acted like they had evidence against him but they didn't. He had a public defender. He couldn't do too much for real. Our word doesn't mean anything. They put it on him. If you don't got nothing on tape – these days, if you ain't got nothing on tape or nothing on video, you got nothing.

Duane: Say you are in narcotics, for instance. They are like the detectives, those sergeants and lieutenants – they all run around with each other in expensive cars, riding around and they are jumping out on people. They probably jump out and when they see you again they try to tackle you or pop you or something and put the cuffs on you. Even though it's a waste of paperwork, they still try to write you up, throw you into booking for like a day, give you a court date. They do it for nothing, just to hassle you. They really get away with whatever they want because we can't do too much.

Isaiah: Go on strike? That ain't going to work. They'll shut it down immediately. Protests? Not happening. We ain't got no say in what goes on when it comes to the police. Police can do whatever they want.

Duane: The lawyers are basically working with [the police]. A lawyer is the most sheistiest. Think about it. He gets paid from both ways. He gets paid from the client. He gets paid from his company. He gets paid from the police, at times and then who do you got to defend you? The lawyer's the sheistiest.

But I don't really feel like I have to be looking over my shoulder. I feel that if you got a certain rep in your neighborhood, you should be all right. You should be all right because people know you. You're known somewhere - not known for doing nothing dumb or something - just known. People know you.

Isaiah: Your best friend could rob you, kill you, you don't know. Hate is everywhere, you feel me? I feel like I can't be around someone I trust totally, like I have to really know you for real. Because a lot of people in this world are phony. They really are phony.

DELORIS

Right now, the justice system is just screwed. Sheila Dixon got in office and now she has police running around like banshees with their head cut off. They're going around harassing people – for what? You know what I'm saying? They're just using their power because they can. Well, you need to be taking out the kingpin of the drugs and stuff. But you don't go around harassing people, like "Get off the corner."

The purpose is giving records and stuff - for what? Just so you can say this was a savage black teen and we changed him. No, you didn't change anybody. And then even when you do that to a certain person, it's hard to come back from that.

TARENA

I have a problem with the police department. They locked my brother up because they thought he was somebody named Terrance Holly just because he looked like the person and they kept him. They didn't ask for his name or his social security. They locked him up, *then* asked him. He had to stay for two days. That's crazy. And like the police officers raping young ladies. That's not cool. It was on the news. They taser people, like when we had the riot out here [in the Southside Academy football field] they wasn't supposed to taser us or nothing.

They could try to change it. Give us - we, the people - more money. As a whole. Also, find the drugs – stop letting the drugs out. They can get rid of all the drugs. Stop growing weed plants.

What are we going to do? They're not going to listen to us because we're kids.

MCINTOSH

The government should make it easier for young people to get more jobs. Then that would make life better because when a kid don't have nothing to do, he'll just go outside and get in trouble, do dumb stuff. When you're young, ain't nothing to do, you go outside and play, but the older you get, the more dangerous stuff you do, I guess. When you're four, you go outside, you don't think about selling drugs or robbing something. When you're like nineteen or eighteen, yeah.

I think it's kind of hard to get jobs now because most places will give you the run-around. They will ask you a lot of questions like have you ever been in trouble with the law. And if you lie, it will make things worse, so you got to tell the truth. And they don't want anybody to work for them if they've been in trouble. You got to be in school. I think if they just made it easier for young people to get jobs, that would be better, instead of harassing you when you look like you're doing drugs.

This has happened to me a couple times. I'd just be sitting on my home boy steps. I mean, I wear jeans and a T-shirt, but that doesn't give them the right to just come and "Spread 'em." I guess it's because it's the neighborhood. I kind of shrugged it off. I knew I was in the right. I was just chillin', right? So I just kind of shrugged it off.

MALCOLM

The police are some crooked people, man. I have had this happen, man. I'm walking down the street at 9:00 at night time and the police jumped out and started choking me. They jumped out of the car and took all of my money out of my pockets, and kept it, took my jewelry, all of it. I didn't do nothing to nobody. They asked my name and nothing and they didn't arrest me. Told me to go on. They just took all my stuff. There's too many crooked police. They took my money, my watch, all of that. But you know me, I got it back.

Tasering. That stuff hurts. I've been shot, tasered, stabbed. Man, it's rough. Cherry Hill is crazy. They smoke drugs and pop pills. It's crazy, man. They should lock up the drug dealers, not the fiends. The police are the ones selling us the drugs so they can kill us. I've seen it on *The Wire*. They know what's going on in Baltimore. I see it on the streets with my own two eyes.

SARAI

Just the other day I was thinking about writing a letter to the mayor because there's a lot of things that's going on in the world. Like I have a boyfriend and something happened in his household - like his father got shot, but he's okay. And somebody hit my boyfriend with a gun and stuff. They was at the police station and my boyfriend, he got locked up previously and they said if he knew anything and he didn't tell them, they was going to lock him up. But he was a victim. He was a victim. And I was going to write to the mayor because I didn't understand - why are things like they are in Baltimore City? And I was just thinking like if I live somewhere else, would it be different?

MIGUEL

I'm going to tell you what someone told me. An officer told me this. He said half of the cops you see really are not from Baltimore City, haven't lived in Baltimore City. It's like the Baltimore City Police Department is hiring like crazy and they're getting people from New York City, Pennsylvania. And they're telling them about Baltimore City up there – and they're looking at us like, they're looking at us like there's no hope for Baltimore City. So they're like okay, I'm going to go and be a cop in Baltimore City. And their mentality coming from New York and Pennsylvania, and Philadelphia is like okay, I'm going to deal with kids that's thirteen, fourteen and fifteen with smart attitudes, mouth off and all this other stuff. And they're getting here and they come with an attitude like knowing what we're going to be about, but we're really not like that.

And you can tell the difference between a Baltimore City cop - a person who lived here his whole life and then became a Baltimore City cop - from someone who haven't lived here all their life. I have saw officers who say, come on guys, let's just get off the corner. I don't want to arrest anybody tonight. Because it's a high traffic area, as in a lot of people hang around that area and they know drugs are in the area - they want to clear the corners. So they can keep a better eye and that's why they put the cameras up on the corner just to see who are the main problems in an area.

But you got some guys who it's hard for them to get a job,

so why lock them up? Why don't you just help them? And see, that's what some officers do. They help them. It's a program called "Get Out of the Game, Stay Out of the Game." That program, that helps you get out of the game, gets you a job, a GED. The YSO officers, Youth Service Officers, started it and that whole unit, they work together and they go out on the streets with their black shirts that say, you know, 'Get Out of the Game." They walk up to people that's standing on the corner and they say, "Do you want to get out of the game?" And it's a yes or no question - they just help you get out of the game.

But you got some officers who would rather see you in jail than at work. So, those are some of the cops who just got that mentality of "Today I'm going to arrest me some people."

I got stopped by the police once, but mine went a different turn when the officer found out I was a Police Explorer. It like turned it around. I was with my captain of the police and I'm a sergeant and me and him were sitting and we're, you know, we're driving down the road and our advisor is in front of us. He is a police officer. And he gets stopped at the red light. We pull into a apartment complex, turn around and wait for him to come from the light, and he takes off up the street and we're following behind him and a police car was behind him. We got in front of the police car and they pulled us over, guns all in our face, lights all in our face. He thought we did a drug deal and they saw us coming out that apartment complex. They saw us pull in and they saw us come out. And it shocked them when we pulled out our IDs and showed him that we were part of the Explorers. We showed them and they were like a big shock on their face and they were like okay, we're sorry, just try to slow down and think about it. They knew we were from their district.

It would have been different [if we weren't Explorers]. It would have been different.

Gangs in Baltimore

One day in early spring, students walking into Anna Stone's tenth grade English class were clearly preoccupied with an incident they had heard about in the hallways. A middle school student over on the west side of Baltimore had been seriously injured in a fight that the media had labeled "gang-related." One of Anna's students - Aquira – thought that the victim might have been her cousin. So Anna decided to set aside her lesson for that day and allow her students to verbally process their feelings and perspectives. The discussion – recorded below – covered a range of topics from why youth join gangs and influences of rap music to relationships with parents and believing in oneself.

Stone: So what happened Aquira?

Aquira: OK, what happened is - I don't want to talk about it.

Kim: They said something about West Baltimore Middle.

Aquira: All right. I'm going to tell you what happened. What I think happened. All right. What happened was there was one kid that had on some red and white Nikes, got banked by at least 20 students, and I think it was my cousin Eric.

Stone: Why did he get banked by twenty students?

Aquira: Because he had red shoes on and they thought he was affiliated with Bloods. Oh boy.

(Silence)

Aquira: Only three of them went to jail.

Deairra: Why only three?

Aquira: Because they only found three.

Deairra: They didn't show his face on the news? He was too scared?

Aquira: His face was probably messed up. If twenty people banged me –

Deairra: But think about it, twenty people on one person you don't get all them hits in.

Aquira: But they stomped him.

Stone: How do you guys feel about not being able to wear a pair of sneakers with a red stripe on it?

Deairra: That don't make no sense. I dress the way I want. I wear red all the time, I wear blue sometimes, once in a blue moon.

Charles: Basically I don't care what I wear. I just wear what I wear and that's it.

Deairra: You catch me in green all the time.

Aquira: Excuse me, can I ask you [looking at Eric] a question real quick? Why do you want to be a gang member?

Why do you want to be a Blood?

Eric: I don't be a gangbanger.

Aquira: Gang *member*. I don't think you're ever going to be a gangbanger.

(Laughter)

Eric: You call my mother you all. You find out.

Stone: So Kim, why would anybody want to be in a gang?

Kim: 'Cause some people are just retarded, they don't got nothing else to do with their life.

Aquira: But some people want attention too. And they think they hard.

Deairra: I think the reason why people join a gang is because of family reasons. They feel loved. If they got nobody else, that's who they're with.
If you really sit down, the gangbangers are intellectuals. If you notice, a lot of gangbangers are actually smarter than they appear to be. So if you really sit down and have a conversation with them they will tell you that the reason why I joined this gang is because they're family.

Stone: So what's the difference between being in a gang, a gang member, a gangbanger and being affiliated?

Kim: Affiliated is you just hang around them. But you

still could have knowledge of what they do.

Stone: So we're all affiliated then.

Aquira: No I'm not affiliated.

Stone: So am I affiliated too?

Kim: No Ms. Stone.

Stone: Oh dang. I feel left out. I don't think that's fair.

Deirra: Do you have friends who are Bloods and Crips?

Stone: [I have] students.

Deairra: No, we're not your friends, we're your students.

Aquira: I think people in Baltimore city are just fakes, I really do. You know how you hear about people from California come down here to G-check people?

Stone: What does it mean to G-check somebody?

Deairra: To ask you about your information, make sure you know what you repping.

Kim: And if you don't know – they beat you.

Deairra: People from California come and take your heads off. They don't "beating" nothing.

Aquira: I actually met a Crip from California. You know my mother drives cabs and everything. He be telling her everything. I'm dead serious. People down here don't even be born in a gang. They just get arrested.

But can I tell you my personal experience when I was living with my father, living on West Baltimore and Gwynns Falls Parkway and Merrow. This one girl named Asia, right? She from RNG, don't know what that is. She hit me in the eye, right, when I was halfway asleep on the bus. I was going to Lemmel, a crazy school. So I was half asleep. And her sister came over and they dap me up. Before she did that, I thought they was cool. Before I turned around, I just saw black and white.

Kim: What does that mean?

Deairra: She hit her.

Aquira: So I tried to fight back. I did the best I could do. When I got tired, I started dipping. Hold on, listen. Because her oldest sister, who I think went to Douglass [High School], was supposed to be in a gang and the only way to be in a gang was if she fought me. It was crazy. That was my first gang experience. It hurt.

Deairra: I had a gang situation, my cousin, who - no names - she was twelve and she was raped by a boy and the boy he raped her so he could be in a gang. So when she went to the police - because her mother thought it was her that let the boy in her house but he snuck through the window - so when they went to the police and told them, his sister found out. His sister wanted to fight her and they still hold that grudge now and the girl about to be eighteen.

Stone: How old was she when that happened?

Deairra: She was twelve. They still hold that grudge to this day and they live in the same neighborhood. I don't know what gang he was trying to get in but he did it so he could be in a gang. He repeatedly raped her all night until the morning time.

Kim: I don't want to hear this.

Aquira: You know like they say one out of every three kids been raped before? If that's true there are ten people here who been raped.

Stone: Ten people at Southside?

(Laughter)

Aquira: Somebody over here, somebody over here.

Deairra: I don't believe in statistics like that when they say one out of three and all that because [it depends on] if you group some people together. It's like one out of four people got AIDS. Anybody here got AIDS? OK then.

Aquira: That's like if you have three virgins, they say one out of three virgins got AIDS and none of them had sex before.

Stone: So Deairra said that mainly it's family issues or problems that people have in their family that make people join a gang. What kind of problems could somebody possibly have in their family to make them want to be part of a gang?

Deairra: Needs and attention, or lack of discipline.

Charles: They may not have good relationship with their parents.

Deairra: If you think about it - I want to say something, this might sound two-sided but being in a gang also help you learn stuff too. But if you know about gang stuff, or you are affiliated with it, gangs teach you - what's it called? Obedience, teach you discipline. It teach you sign language, being in a gang, it do help you a little bit, but in a negative way just like when Major Colbert asked us, what is the definition of a leader. Anybody can be a leader, even if you're a leader in a negative way you still influence people. You got the ability to lead 'cause they still listen to you.

Stone: But what kind of issues at home would make a person want to be part of a gang?

Aquira: Some people like probably Deairra was saying want to impress their family. Say if I have a older sister who thinks I'm a chump and all that and then next thing you know she see me wearing a red flag or a pink flag going around and doing dumb stuff. Then she think you got all hard. Gang members do stuff that's just neutral, it's not even anything.

Stone: So sometimes they do it to impress their siblings. What about what Charles said? What did you say Charles?

Charles: They have problems with their parents. Say if the son or daughter is arguing with their parents, like saying I can't handle this no more, I'm going to go do something. That's probably one of the causes for them joining.

Stone: So not having a positive relationship with your

parents. How many of you know people who don't have a good relationship with their parents?

Charles: I don't think anybody has a good relationship with their parents.

Eric: But there are other ways to get around that. If you have other family like that, you just go live with them. You might have a good relationship with your grandmother. Better than your mother.

Stone: So just because you have a bad relationship with your parents doesn't necessarily mean you're going to join a gang, is that what you were trying to say Eric?

Deairra: The gang thing is played out for me.

Stone: So why do you think it's so popular? I know a lot of people come to school and - What does a black rag mean?

Deairra: Everything, it just depends on what side you on.

Stone: Why is it, when you said it was the song that made it popular...

Deairra: We didn't say that. We said that's when it came out, about that same time, Bow-wow started the Crip walk and Shug Knight told him he was going to break his legs.

Stone: So you don't think that that song had an impact? Like you were saying music influences teenagers to do certain things.

Deairra: I said it doesn't, I don't think so.

Aquira: I know one time when it influenced somebody. I think it was one of those Jim Jones songs or Game. Some music make people want to be gangmembers. Some of it really do. As much as that statement sounds biased. It really do.

Stone: *How* do you think music influences -

Aquira: Not music, but some songs. I told you Game or Jim Jones, they be saying Blood this, Blood that. You got some people out there saying that they are a Blood, who got no affiliation, they don't know nothing, no knowledge.

Ismail: The music starts an epidemic. You know that Nelly song *Grills* - that song came out and everybody started getting grills and stuff.

Stone: OK the grills, the fronts in their mouth. Who had a song about Air Force Ones [basketball shoes], was that Nelly? Even when I was a teenager, we had Run DMC and they talked about My Adidas. Everybody wore Adidas. Everybody wore Adidas sweatsuits.

Deairra: There's a difference between a fashion style and gang banging. When I say it doesn't influence you to do something stupid. In the songs it's not telling you all go shoot somebody. It's not saying go bang somebody. It's not telling you what tennis shoes to wear. It's talking about them wearing tennis shoes.

Eric: Tupac, 36 Mafia, they're talking about busting people's heads and all that. That could start something.

Stone: They used to in a lot of their music. I lived in Memphis and a lot of their music [36 Mafia] used to start big brawls in the club – "Tear the Club Up Thugs."

Deairra: Only crazy people - I'm not going to call them stupid – but only crazy people will go out and listen to a song and say I'm going to shoot somebody tomorrow in the head because TI or Lil' Wayne told me to.

Stone: There was a court case in Atlanta where a young man who had listened to Tupac went out and shot a police officer. He said he had been listening to his song about…

Deairra: That's just an excuse. People use it as an excuse to get out of what they are doing. I don't believe that a normal person in their right state of mind will listen to a song and then will up and change their whole personality or their whole "them."

Lakeda: Stuff gets stuck in your head.

Deairra: I listen to love songs all the time. Do I talk about love all the time?

Eric: Yeah.

Aquira: I know when I listen to C-Murder, I feel real dangerous like I'm going to hurt somebody. Round my way where I used to live at, you know where Lakeland is? I don't like nobody around that neighborhood. When I listen to C-Murder, I just want to go kill somebody.

Stone: Why do you think that's the case that you want to go kill somebody?

Aquira: It's a murder song.

Stone: What are some of the words?

Aquira: It's just, you know he killed somebody before and then he got off for that. You know in that song he talks about how he shot people, how he sold drugs. That don't make me want to sell drugs because that's just not me, but it might make me want to go kill somebody.

Stone: OK, so I think I'm getting it now. So when you hear a rapper expressing some of the same sentiments that you have about people in your neighborhood, maybe he's expressing some of the same anger. It kind of makes you connect and relate. You're like "Oh, I'm really feeling that."

Aquira: Not saying I would listen to him and then go kill someone. It just makes me feel like that. I wouldn't really go kill someone.

Stone: So you believe if someone were in a weaker state of mind, they would go out after listening to that?

Deairra: Even if you were in your weak state of mind – oh my goodness, it makes me so mad. How can you let a song determine what you gonna do? Before that song came out you was doing you. You wasn't robbing nobody; you wasn't killing nobody.

Eric: I was doing me.

Randall: If you go to sleep and play a certain song and by the time you wake up you most likely remember what the words was.

Ismail: Young kids, when they listen to songs, say it could be like your favorite artist saying stuff like, "Yeah I used to do this and that's how I got rich." I think young kids just want to follow suit.

Stone: 'Cause they see the money?

Lakeda: I know in the world you have to have money to go places. I don't care about money because if I don't got it, I just don't have it. It just don't matter to me.

Stone: You're just not willing to do some of the things that other people do for money.

Deairra: They make money seem like it's the best thing in the world. And after we watched that movie that you showed us Miss Stone? Money has no value. Soon as I have enough money I'm going to invest. I saw on the news that license plates with single digits in Detroit is a good investment because people want to buy that or something. It's crazy how money has no value but things does. Like how a home builds equity.

Stone: And we just have to know where to invest our money, we just can't buy clothes all the time or grills or whatever we spend our money on.

Charles: For people who invest they got to do their homework on it so they know if it goes down they're going to lose money. The stock market is the main place you might not want to invest your money cause it can go down really bad. You can lose a ton of money. I'd rather invest money in a dealership that's going to be gaining more money than lose it. I'd rather put my money in a good business that's going to make it through. The stock market - it's a 50/ 50 chance your money is going up.

Deairra: I'm going to invest in myself.

Stone: In what ways can you invest money in yourself?

Deairra: Building myself up, just like when I watched the documentary about Destiny's Child. Their father put all that money away when the sisters had no diapers, just so they could move and travel. And look where they are now? Look what they have now- money.

Stone: So sacrifice.

Deairra: That's what I was trying to tell my mother - Mom if you really believe in my vocals you should give up everything we got.

Stone: Go ahead, we got one minute - sing.

Deairra: Oh no, that will never happen.

Stone: You have to believe in *yourself* Deairra.

And a lot of people have told me don't give up. You can be anything you put your mind to. You could do anything. Don't let nobody never tell you you can't do. Keep your head up. It's rough out here for us. Keep your head up.
AARON C.

When you see everybody else's life, [you] don't realize you just see the outside. Like in school. People have good grades, but at home they probably don't eat. You see the outside of the shell and when you see the inside of it, then you can really understand how it is. **LAJUANE**

In America, they say we don't appreciate, but you go down to [the Dominican Republic] and you got to sleep on the floor and you got to wash up in un-sterilized water. It teaches you to appreciate where you come from. **MIGUEL**

MIGUEL

Listening to Miguel. *In the ninth grade, before taking the Algebra High School Assessment Miguel told his Algebra teacher, "We need a prayer circle this morning for this test." He conducted the prayer along with all the students in the class who eagerly participated. They stood in the hallway and formed their circle and he prayed.*

During many class discussions Miguel would reference the Bible and was not ashamed of his religious background. He lived with his grandparents and it was evident that his grandparents were a great influence on him. He conducted himself like a young man who was much older. Not because he was mature but because it was expected. He had his days when he chose to be like the others. He and Macintosh would talk about each other. "Macintosh, Ms. Stone said people with no neck can't talk in class today. So shut up."

I went down to the Dominican Republic with Youth for Christ. We have different teams. We have the construction team, we have the medic team, and we have the vacation Bible school team and we go down there and we serve. We serve, we give our time to all the kids and the people in the church. And we went to this place called Pimentel. It was about two days into our trip and we went to a little - I forgot what it's called - but when we went in that town, we had to get off the bus because they were still building the bridge to go across. There was a little bridge, but a truck couldn't go over. So we had to get off the bus, walk down and just take all our briefcases and suitcases full of medicine to the town. We had to walk to the town. It was a lot of supplies. I had two suitcases, you know, we didn't have no roller suitcases, so I was carrying two suitcases and once we got everything set up, people started swarming in to come get medicine and different things for their kids.

And later we saw these same people running down the street and we were like what's going on? And then it was as though we were there at the right time because a one year old, he fell off a 50' cliff into the water and we started running and we saw all these people going in this one house and we went around the back and we saw everybody just jumping off the cliff to save the little boy. And the doctor heard the baby cry and he said, well that's a good sign because he's still alive. So they brung the baby up and we got him some medicine and got the water out of his chest. There was no other doctor in town. The nearest clinic is about four miles in town.

It was a powerful experience because what if we wasn't there, you know? And I was so glad that we were there at the right moment and all of the people that were down there, they were so happy that we were there at that time and it got even worse because a lady passed out. She thought it was her child. We had to go help her and him and it was a lot of stuff we had to do.

It taught me to appreciate. In America, they say we don't appreciate, but you go down there and you got to sleep on the floor and you got to wash up in un-sterilized water. It teaches you to appreciate where you come from. A lot of them were like, "We want to go back with you guys." And it's hard. Money down there can go like that (snaps fingers). And you got nothing.

The whole time I was down there, I was like I really do appreciate America. I really do appreciate where I come from because in the Dominican you have people living in houses that's broken up and they say that some people got to leave their houses halfway built because they have a law. If your house is fully built, you have to pay ground taxes and land taxes. And a lot of people don't got that money so they halfway build the houses so they don't have to pay it - it won't have a lot of walls, no windows, even like curtains hanging, filling in the hole and, you know, the porch is halfway done.

And they get their water pumped from the city and it takes six hours to get to the city. They pump the water through the city line and then some people order water from the truck that comes out from the city and gives the whole town water. In our particular town, when we washed up, we couldn't open our mouths because a couple years ago, a cow had died in their sewer hole. Kids were playing in there while the cow was still in there and the feces, so they had to clean that all out. And they couldn't get it clean, so they told us not to open our mouth. We had to tape it shut.

And that really affected me. That made me appreciate stuff.

TARENA

The best advice that I had was never look back in the past. My best friend said that to me. Don't look back on the bad stuff. I used to hold grudges on people for a long time. Like I held a grudge on my mother because she wasn't never there and she won't come around now. And I'm so mad about it I don't speak to her or nothing now. When they say don't look back on the past, I guess it means that you can't change what's already happened. Or, don't be still mad, just try and make it better. I agree with this advice because it is true. Like, you can't change the past because it's already happened. All you can do is look forward and focus on the future.

GAGE

I look up to myself because if you look up to somebody else, then you're going to think that's who you want to be and you should be yourself and do what you want to do. Whatever's right in your mind.

DEINERA

Well, honestly, if I feel like somebody's trying to destroy me, or diminish my spirit, I'm going to let you know quick how I feel. However you think it, that is what it is, that's the attitude I've got. But sometimes, just like people tell me, I've got to humble myself. So I would handle that situation by just saying "You've got to love yourself because if you don't, who will?" I don't say it out loud, but to myself. It will get me over it.

TORI

My mother gives me all my good advice. One of the things that she told me not to do, that's really helped me out, is not to hide my talent. Sometimes people hide anything that's good that's going on with them. Like if you're really smart – I think I'm pretty smart – and you hide it. There's somebody in the class that does that. I'm not going to say their name, though. If you hide your talent -because you might be scared that your classmates call you geek and stuff like they call me "History Channel" - if I were to hide my intellect, then I'd fail the class, caring about what they say.

HEATH

I was working on this short story about a guy - I think the story starts off with him being buried in the sand up to his neck and the guy next to him is buried too. It's like some Amazonian tribe that did it and he turns and there's a dude next to him just sitting there. And then as the story goes along, he realizes it's God there with him. But at first he doesn't know and he goes through the whole story trying to get to this jungle and there's God next to him, with him, and God does everything to mess him up, putting him through all the hardships - because this ties into why the man left. He has a family back home. He went to the Amazon to find himself and the experience teaches him to be patient with his family. Like he's trying to start a fire and then God slips and knocks sand into the fire and puts it out and he doesn't know it's God. He thinks it's just a dude that was buried next to him. When they had just gotten out of the sand God goes over and starts to build a sandcastle. "Why are you going to do that?" says the man, "We need to get out of here." It's beautiful.

I don't believe in God, but I put him in my story because I thought he'd be funny. Obviously, God has humor. Not saying he would be a clown or a jester, but he obviously has to have a sense of humor and I thought who would have a better sense of humor than God? Who would see the funny in everything, you know? I think some people take God a little too seriously. God would have to have a sense of humor to put up with us. Seriously.

But I don't believe in God. Well, I believe in God. I just don't believe in religion, worshiping God and what not. I mean, why would he want me to worship him? I think we're his little test subjects. I think we're his mistake gone wrong.

"Oh look at that. That's cool, that piece of fungus is growing on that thing and it's a human civilization."

And I read the Bible. The Bible influenced me in writing that story because there's a section after Eve eats the apple and Adam hides from God while he's walking to the garden, and God says why are you hiding? Adam says because I'm naked. And God says, who told you you're naked? So obviously, there is some sense of knowledge there that we have now. It wasn't the apple. The apple wasn't bad. The apple wasn't bad because the apple was knowledge. The Bible gives apples a bad view. Apples are delicious. And knowledge is delicious, too, delicious for your mind.

Religion to me is overrated. It holds people back. It's judgmental. It gives you bad views of other people when you should just learn who that person is and love the person for who they are instead of their religion and stuff. Like the different Muslim denominations fighting each other. And the different Christian denominations. I mean, why would you spread it up and break it into these pieces, you know? It's just ridiculous because it all goes back to the same thing, the same place. Why? I don't understand.

LAJUANE

Listening to Lajuane. *Lajuane is a bright young man who has lived a tough life. Life has made him tough and cynical. I met him in my 9th grade English class and saw that he challenges authority when he sees inconsistency, phoniness and insecurity. He is a thinker and will make you think. His questions, responses and defiance will cause you to reflect on your own behavior and teaching. He is observant and analytical but he is way too cool and way too smart for* *his own good and for school.*

"I know this stuff. I know I know it. You don't know I know it. Why I gotta show you? My learning is for me right? It ain't for you. Who are you? Why I gotta prove somethin' to you? I'm not doing this."

What could I say? I reasoned that it was about grades and if I didn't know or if he didn't show that he knew then he wouldn't get the grade and wouldn't graduate.

"That's dumb. Grades don't mean nothin'." he replied.

"Well Lajuane, I didn't create the system, I just work it and you better learn how to work it too."

There was no winning with Lajuane.

It's the ability to understand information that you need to process that gets you to learn what you need to learn. Because if you don't get the information, or the right information, you're stuck. It's like steps. That's what Coach Russell - he taught us in middle school on the basketball court - it's like school is in steps. Basically, it's like walking up the steps. Every time you walk up the steps, you need to put another foot in front of the foot before it. So basically you're taking another step higher than it was before, but basically you're doing the same thing, no matter what. It's just higher. You can't skip a step and think you're going to get to the next one without that one. And like he said, it's rare that you will see somebody don't graduate or get education and still be successful. Even them that is successful, they still went through hardships, tribulations to get where they're at because it couldn't have been easy for them. If it was, then really nobody would have to go to school.

A couple teachers here at Southside have been through what I've been through. Like Ms. Stone, from what I can tell, Ms. Stone went through it.

Mr. J--, he grew up where I grew up at, in the same neighborhood. No matter what kind of life you grew up in, you're always going to have problems and it might not be the same situation, but everybody has problems in their house, mental problems. Some people can have stuff and still not be happy. And some people can be happy and be broke.

I think happiness is a mindset. Happiness is what you make it because you decide in your mind whether you're happy or not. When people say how they affect other peoples' self-esteem, I don't really get it because however they perceive you, you take it in your mind and you process it the way you see it. Like if you insulted me or told me something about my clothes, it's up to my mind to process it and bring myself down like I can't do nothing about it, or take that and build on that information to try to get better. I think of it as other people, they try to affect your feelings, happiness or emotions in any kind of way. They affect it, but it's just advice. Yeah, I take it as advice. They're advising you. That's it. They're advising. They can't tell you to do nothing. They can only advise you. So then you make your own happiness.

Where we're born in America, we got our choices. Like in Africa, some of them can't even have a choice to be happy because they got to do certain stuff when they're little so they can't live a life that they need or that they would want, but us, we really don't got responsibilities other than going to school. Even like the stuff I've been through, I never thought of it as real bad because I knew it could have been worse. I could have been homeless or something. I know some people probably homeless or in group homes or stuff like that, and I'm fortunate I never had to go through that. So that's how I'll always think of it – it could have been worse than my situation. Everybody's situation could have been worse and just think of it as if you was a step below, like how I was living with my coach. Obviously I could have been in foster care. That would have been worse. That's when you don't – you don't have a choice. You have to be there. I had a choice of where I wanted to go. That's how I think of it.

Anything could have happened to me. We could have burnt the house down cooking, anything. Any natural thing could have happened. And by us living in the projects, there was shooting. A person could have tried to run in our house when he was getting chased by the police and we could have even got involved in that. But fortunately it didn't happen.

People usually look at the bad stuff because you see everybody else's life, and don't realize you just see the outside. You don't never see it as it is because you don't live with that person or you don't be with them. But if you follow a person around, then you already know what they're going through. Like in school. People have good grades, but at home they probably don't eat. They probably got to work, but they come here and you'll never know it. Or they could come here and be all bad and run the halls and you go to their house and they've got seven rooms and four cars or something. But it's just the shell. You see the outside of the shell and when you see the inside of it, then you can really understand how it is.

There ain't one person that's perfect because if they was, they wouldn't be here. Here meaning earth, not just Southside. If they was perfect, they would be in heaven and they would be an angel or something. And by you being surrounded by people that's got problems, you will always have problems because their problems influence you.

MALCOLM

Time is money. Don't play around with time because it's about money. *Church!* If you waste time, you're wasting money because, if you go to work late, all right, they fire you. You wasted time, now you ain't got no money because you were late. ***Church!*** You can't do nothing without no money.

I don't know. It depends on how your health is. But you need money for your health so money is the most important thing. Can I hear a ***Church***? Another piece of advice is to use your head for more than a hat rack. Some old dude from downtown said that to me. I don't know what he was talking about, but he said it. Use your head for more than just putting hats on your head or something. Be smart. Be wise. When there's a will, there's a way.

MCINTOSH

I think the best piece of advice I was ever told was when Coach Mobley told me not to give up. He's the football coach. My freshman year I came and I wasn't that good of a football player. I was - I ain't going to say overweight - but yeah, I was kind of overweight, and not muscular or anything. I just came. I tried to get like more exercise and get better 'cause I wanted to play football. I watched it on TV and I tried to play it in high school. My first couple of weeks I wasn't doing anything right, forgetting plays. One day he pulled me aside, and said just don't give up, 'cause I was going to quit. He said don't give up, keep going, you got to finish what you start, just keep going for it. I really thought about what he said. I went home that day and really thought about what he said and I stayed. I got stronger and faster, toned down a little bit. I lost a little bit of weight, I guess.

AARON C.

The most important thing that has happened to me is that I'm still living and that's helping me make a change in my life. Started off on the wrong foot, ended up on the right foot. I didn't want to go to school. I failed twice and I realized my little brother - we're two years apart - he caught up with me. We're both in the twelfth grade this year. And that motivated me, I mean, if he could do it, I could do it too. We both came from the same mother, not the same father, though. But we live in the same house, and I should be able to do it too.

And a lot of people have told me don't give up. You can be anything you put your mind to. You could do anything. Don't let nobody never tell you you can't do. Keep your head up. It's rough out here for us. Keep your head up. Keep focused. You'll get through it. You can't find a way – go to church. Lord will help you get through it. Don't get caught up in the wrong crowd. Don't hang with the wrong crowd. I've got a bright future. A lot of people believe in me so I've got to believe in myself. I heard that so many times I had to listen to it.

What Urban Youth Need from Adults

The thirty-four young people who speak out in these pages are amazing and ordinary. In some ways, they are "typical teenagers;" in other ways, they defy generalizations. To say that "a lot of stuff is going on" in their lives, as Saraii and Darious put it, is an understatement. It is challenging enough to manage communication and relationships with parents, peers, members of the opposite sex, teachers, and the police; but our urban teens are also faced with a pile of paradoxes. In their narratives, we hear their expectations to be treated as capable, independent-minded individuals and simultaneously feel their hesitation to be completely on their own. Meanwhile, some of them carry adult responsibilities to care for their parents or younger siblings, to get jobs that will pay for their clothes, and to "take precautions" to avoid getting shot or harassed. Janae treasures her freedom but also criticizes her mother for not disciplining her more; Lakeda and Deairra want good friendships, but are leery of the consequences of yielding to peer pressure; Madisen knows that "all boys cheat" but doesn't want to "mess up the next chance" in case a boy really likes her.

We were struck by the number of heavy decisions with which our thirty-four young people wrestle. To have sex or abstain? To have children or not? To get married or "just stay together for a long time?" To get out of Baltimore so you can be influenced by a different environment (Lajuane) or stay because Baltimore is where you "know people," where you "connect" (Deloris)? At times, it seems as if they are burdened by the weightiest of social issues: policies that keep people poor, political corruption and police harassment, satanic influences, whether Barack Obama will be assassinated, being scared to die, and the world coming to an end.

If there is anything we have learned from the process of listening to the Southside students, it is that they are incredibly sensitive to the ways in which they are treated by the adults in their lives. Adults should not be so surprised by this, but the fact that we are suggests that we have largely forgotten – if we were even conscious of it ourselves - the extraordinarily important developmental work that adolescents must engage in. Adolescence is a transition time between childhood and adulthood – the life stage in which one's self-concept must be actively constructed. The self-concept is the sum total of how one organizes a multitude of thoughts and feelings about one's self. It is not static, but can fluctuate depending upon what is happening in one's environment (Erickson, 1968).

The Southside students - like all adolescents – construct their self-concepts by experimenting with persona, weighing values, making social comparisons, and then making adjustments based on the feedback they receive from – guess whom? – teachers, parents, and peers. The self concept that eventually emerges from this process represents in large part what gets reflected back to teenagers from these significant others, thus the phrase "the looking glass self" (Cooley, 1902). Adults may be completely oblivious to the fact that their attitudes, reactions, admonishments and affirmations have major consequences for what the young people in their lives think about themselves. To those of us committed to "doing right by" these young people, it's about time we started to pay attention.

What Urban Youth Need from Their Teachers

City kids may "act hard," but their sensors are always able to pick up on when adults have "given up on them." And "giving up" on urban youth is – as Deinera says – "the worse thing you can do." There is never an excuse in the eyes of these youth for adults – especially teachers – to give up on them. Not if they stop doing homework, not if they skip your class, not even if they cuss at you. They need to perceive that teachers think they are capable of making it. They disdain teachers who appear to treat their jobs as well, *a job*, rather than take on the role of – in Aaron S.'s words – "a second mother or father."

A common refrain in the narratives is a strong desire for support from teachers, for taking more time to make sure students have learned the content *before* giving the test, for inspiring them to find meaning in the content in the first place (Choc - "we like someone to motivate us, for real"), and for "helping out with the other stuff going on" in their lives.

Stories about teachers who mistreat their students strike a raw nerve. During the year we collected these narratives, one of the "most viewed" videos posted on the *Baltimore Sun*'s website featured a fist fight at a local high school between a teenage girl and her female teacher. The incident had been captured on a cell phone and prompted a great deal of public concern about "out of control students." It wasn't until the girl's trial ten months later that the truth came out: students and school officials testified that the teacher had initiated the fight by cursing at the girl and punching her for "getting in her space" (Fenton, February 3, 2009). Southside students were quick to express their outrage at how easily blame is placed on the youth rather than on the adults who are not doing their job.

High school teachers may see any individual student for a fraction of a day – a completely inadequate amount of time to grasp who that student is as a person, as a sibling, as a daughter or son, and the demands on that student's time, emotions and body. As Miguel pointed out to Anna, "Do you even realize that some of us have to wake up at 6:00 in the morning just to risk our lives coming to school, waiting at bus stops, taking three buses to get here. We need your prayers!"

Many Southsiders believe that teachers should care about their students as if they were their own children. School should feel like home, a place where students are seen and heard as individuals, not as categories and types. Teachers need to suspend judgment – set aside unconscious assumptions – until they have given their students a chance to show what makes each of them tick. As Aaron S. admonished, "Don't assume that everyone without a father is affected by that. Some of us are; some of us aren't."

They probably won't show it, but most of the youth we listened to have internalized the message that getting an education is essential to their future success, though for some "getting an education" is equated with abstract grades and diplomas rather than developing a solid academic identity. Even those who rarely attend school talk about respecting teachers who push, who sit you down and make you read about history, who "make sure we know it before you move on" to the next chapter in the textbook. They might get on teachers' nerves – but they would rather have a "real teacher" than a paraprofessional serving as babysitter because no math or science teacher can be found to replace the one who left. They expect teachers to care so much that even if they misbehave, "no matter how much we mess up," teachers will not quit in the middle of the school year. Students who had been expelled from school like Aaron C., Darious, and Choc seem to interpret their expulsion as a personal rejection: "I felt like the school system was letting me down" (Aaron C.).

The Southside students are also quite ready to debate the question of how they might ***prove*** their learning. After all, it is obvious to them whether they learned something or not. Does passing a single test prove you learned something? Should someone's whole future be determined by a test required for graduation? What do grades really prove? Are they bogus? Everyone knows kids that were passed on even though they didn't learn what they needed to know to succeed in life. Some people have test anxiety, but then again, maybe teenagers should take responsibility and do more studying on their own, as Tori suggests.

Instinctively, teachers may react merely to teenagers' surface persona, the protective layer of toughness or indifference which obscures who our teenagers really are. Teachers must be ever conscious of the fact that what adolescents show on the outside is not what's going on in the inside. If all teachers perceive is that hardness, they may respond in kind, rather than meet their students where they are on the inside. The developmental work of adolescence requires that teenagers "display different selves in different social contexts, struggling to reconcile these differences as well as determine 'the real me'" (Harter, 1990, p. 355). What teachers see in any one day does not tell the whole story. An adolescent's behavior may change from hour to hour as she or he responds to different teachers and new social situations.

This means that teachers have to be incredibly mature and able to react to teenager behavior differently than they might react to the same behavior in adults. Teachers have to treat each day as a new day, let go of whatever happened the previous day, don't hold their students' mistakes over their heads. Teachers can't take what students say or do personally because often they don't know what else is going on in a student's life. A student might be mad about something that happened outside of school; punishing him for acting out that anger in school is not going to address the larger issues.

Take Darious for example. When Darious was a freshman, he never did his homework and often tuned out during class. He became quite irritated and agitated if Anna reprimanded him verbally. But Anna also provided opportunities for her students to reveal aspects of their lives in journals – which they wrote in during class time – and so she learned that Darious harbored deep feelings of rejection and neglect because he perceived that his father loved his sister more than him. So she knew that the message Darious most needed from her was the message that Darious was lovable no matter what he did.

Sometimes teachers may have to apologize to their students. One day Deinera took Anna's bag and slung it on the floor. Anna lost it for a moment and yelled at Deinera, saying things that she soon regretted. At the end of the class period, Anna asked Deinera to stay behind and apologized for swearing at her. In typical teenager fashion – not wanting to let any sort of feelings show – Deinera replied "Ms. Stone, ain't nobody thinking about you." But that was OK. Anna knew that the apology would earn Deinera's respect.

Too many teachers get caught in the belief that consistency means administering identical consequences each and every time an infraction occurs. This is bound to backfire. Instead, on the first day of class each fall, Anna explicitly tells her students not to expect her to treat everyone exactly the same. "I'm going to treat you as the unique individuals you are." This means that Anna had to choose her battles with someone like William whose anger was on a hair-trigger, who regularly laced his sentences with "fuck" and "shit," but who did his work when he was feeling calm and showed up for class. One day he might stand up and yell "I don't give a fuck about this class" and walk out, but return the next day ready to do his work. Anna's approach was to welcome him to class, tell him that it was not OK for him to cuss, but that she was glad to see him and let it go at that. It is not that she wouldn't punish William – she called his mother and detained him after school for skipping class - but not for cussing. Cussing was William's way of expressing the intensity of his feelings – it was also practically a way of life for him.

Sometimes, teachers choose to teach in urban classrooms because they feel sorry for city kids and want to save them. This is not what Southside students have in mind when they call for "second parents." The savior mentality is based on a perverse kind of misunderstanding, one that is probably fed by unconscious stereotyping produced by uncritical viewing of the media and images of city kids in popular culture or one's own self-centered need to be a hero. Some of the youth portrayed in this book have led incredibly difficult lives, but the commitment to work with them is a commitment to listen to their reality, not judge it as defeating or debilitating.

"Second parents" pay attention to their students and are cautious about the judgments of other professionals who have not yet learned the importance of listening. Anna describes herself as unapologetically "nosy," eavesdropping on the conversations her students have with each other in order to learn more about who they are, how they react when they're angry, how they express themselves with their body language. She makes a point to join them in the cafeteria for lunch; she doesn't ignore students as she walks by, but calls them by name: "You better come to my class today." And she employs several strategies in the classroom to gain access to her students' emerging self-constructs: writing prompts, the memoir project, interviews.

City teachers who manage to become these "second

parents" face many more professional boundary issues than their counterparts in other settings. It is not uncommon for city teachers to make their cell phone number available in case of emergency, transport students in their own vehicle, even provide meals or shelter on a temporary basis.

What Urban Youth Need from Their Families

Most of the students represented in this book have at least one parent or relative who provides a kind of anchor in their lives and they would very much like those people to know about the good stuff they do in school. Unfortunately, communication between parents and teachers is hindered by a number of factors. In their need for increasing independence, teenagers sometimes send the message to their parents that they should keep their distance. And one of the ways parents may take the path of least resistance is to keep their distance from schools. Teachers are often not given time or space to make contact with parents outside of parent-teacher conferences.

Teenagers may display a "different self" at school than the one they perform at home. Parents – like teachers – have to be mature enough to consider the infinite array of contextual variables that influence an adolescent's behavior: Who's watching? Peers one hopes to impress? Adults one hopes to emulate?

Parents are often preoccupied with making sure their children respect them, but may not realize that once those children become teenagers, that respect has to be reciprocated. Respect for teenagers cannot depend upon good hygiene, conventional appearance, or manners and civility. Respect for teenagers has to come from an acute awareness that they have reached a stage in which they know a whole lot more than we give them credit for, even if they are still immature or impulsive in their actions. When Ashley says that she can be herself at school but not at home, she might be speaking about the discomfort that parents often feel about accepting their child as a differentiated self. Indeed, our contributors' opinions of their parents run the gamut from sources of inspiration (Deairra, Lakeda and Aaron S.) to examples of whom *not* to emulate (Madisen, Janae and Tarena).

If the danger for teachers is trying to be a hero in their students' lives, the temptation for parents is to think of their children as reflections of themselves. Too often, if a child does something wrong, parents become preoccupied with defending their performance as parents rather than accepting their role as a mentor who allows teenagers to find their own way in life. Parents should never doubt that their adolescent son or daughter needs their presence in their lives. Aaron S. couldn't be more blunt: "Just by having a father in your life, it can change your whole concept."

Over and over again, the Southside youth express a desire for open lines of communication with their parents – and the right to determine the content and timing of that communication. The Southside youth also make it clear that they need and want external locus of control. "Make me get up and come to school" and "Don't allow me to spend the night at my boyfriend's house" and "We need to have someone on our back." It takes a careful listener to decipher a son's or daughter's apparently contradictory desire for both freedom and discipline. Janae spells it out: Her mother's discipline may not prevent Janae from having sex, but it's far better than communicating the message that you don't care if she gets hurt or pregnant.

A major issue for parents of teenagers in some of Baltimore's toughest neighborhoods (like Cherry Hill for instance) is dealing with the requirements for survival on the streets. The code of the street is that if someone hits you or challenges you and you don't retaliate with force, you are a punk. You are a victim. An urban teenager experiences many such situations and some get support from their parents to hit back. More than once, Anna has heard a parent tell a child, "If you don't fight back, I'll kick your ass."

There's no question that Southside youth experience life as a struggle, probably due to the inevitable difficulties of adolescence compounded by the ever-present effects of racism and poverty. "Nothing comes easy," says Deinera. You've got to struggle to survive, "because it's a crazy world." Over and over again, we were struck by the optimism and self-confidence with which these young people face adversity. So many of them recognize when others (be it a close friend or society in general) tried to discourage or limit them and they talked about resisting such efforts. "Don't give up." "Believe you've got a bright future." "Don't hide your talents." "Make your own happiness." "Think about people who have it worse than you." Community psychologists have a word to describe adolescents from high-stress communities (like Cherry Hill) who display social and individual competence in spite of the risk factors in their environment: the word is *resilience* (Arrington & Wilson, 2000).

What Urban Youth Need from our Public Institutions

"Government" is an abstract concept to most urban youth, but they perceive it as a kind of conduit of power and they have plenty to say about how power can be used and misused. To put it bluntly, none of our contributors to this book feel "cared about" by government. Whether talking about the mayor, the governor, the state assembly or Congress and the White House, Southside youth perceive that those with political power hold all the wrong priorities. Instead of dealing with homelessness, poverty and under-resourced schools, politicians and government employees are not doing their jobs and protect no one but their own self-interests. Some of our youth have experienced so much police harassment and have seen so many of their relatives and acquaintances arrested that it should not surprise us when Duane asserts that there is no real commitment to end urban violence because the criminal justice system has become a business.

Urban youth may not have much knowledge about the structures and processes of government, but they are likely to hold a healthy skepticism. Deloris stands out as a teenager who regularly reads the newspaper and watches news channels on television, but most Southsiders would agree with her that "the government withholds information" from the public. This is not something that is taught in school – at least it is not part of the official curriculum which is oriented more toward nurturing passivity and conformity than in cultivating any kind of revolutionary thinking. So Southside youth - tuned into the strong undercurrent of discontent in communities experiencing persistent unemployment, high rates of incarceration, and an absence of public investment in infrastructure - are skeptical that public officials have the will to make needed change. As a result, they might conclude, like Lakeda, that "change needs to happen at the local level" or, like Heath, "just depend upon yourself."

The students' criticism covers a lot of territory, but the most strident accusations of government neglect are aimed at public education. The problems with Southside's physical environment are a sore spot. In Deairra's words, "If your school is messed up, you don't feel like coming." They may not complain out loud to their teachers or principals, but that's not for lack of noticing. These young people are keeping a tally: Out-of-date textbooks with torn covers and marked pages; scratched-up doors and graffiti on the walls; broken desks and not enough of them; no computer lab.

When invited to give their input, they have solutions. When high schools are closed down (as Baltimore City started doing in 2007), why aren't their desks and computers distributed to the schools – like Southside – that are required to absorb the additional students? Why couldn't the schools provide free summer school, career counseling, job skills training, driver's education, Chinese and Russian classes, or swimming lessons? Why aren't school officials raising the expectations for a passing grade instead of lowering them? Why can't the people with master's degrees sitting behind a desk in the Baltimore City school administration building or school board members - people who know how to make a school run – come help the principal make Southside better?

It may surprise some Baltimoreans to learn that Baltimore City Public Schools operates a tiered-system, where some high schools receive a larger share of funding and are permitted to deny admission to all but the highest-achieving students. Southside students may have never attended a school outside of Cherry Hill, but they all know about the inequities that exist. Southside is a "poor school" says Tori. Miguel quips: "Where is the federal stimulus package for our school?"

For some urban youth, the blatant inequality in the distribution of resources is part and parcel of racism. Saraii – petite and soft-spoken – doesn't mince words:

> Sometimes the Caucasians get the better service and better things than we do. Like you go in a county school where a lot of Caucasians are at, they got better desks,

> better books, newer stuff, and you come
> to our school and our desks are raggedy.
> I think even Mexicans get better service
> than we do.

And Deairra sees what is at the root of the pain for African-American males who might defy all of the stereotypes about black boys as "drug dealers and gang bangers," and yet who are still "viewed as worthless" by a public so pre-conditioned to see nothing else.

This is a generation of African American youth who have no memory of the Civil Rights Movement or Black Power and for whom few teachers or parents make much effort to cultivate a sense of pride in black history. For them, the campaign and election of President Barack Obama illuminates that lack – they must work backwards from the excitement they see in adults to recognize the historical significance of the 2008 election, the racial uplift. "If Obama can do it, we can too." Without being specific about what they mean by "it," we heard this sentiment frequently in our conversations with the Southside youth.

Yet for many of them, the sentiment is tempered by caution. Yes, celebrate Obama - "Barack all day" (Aaron S.) – and admire his courage, but let's get real. For these young people, Obama's election is not so much a promise that government will be able to change society as it is an important new marker in the long history of black people's struggle for social and economic equality. Like Duane said, "It's still about the money."

But if the Southside youth could convince the mayor of Baltimore to make just one change in priorities, they would call for the focus to be on the Cherry Hill community. The narratives in this book describe a litany of problems, not the least of which is the norm of violence perpetuated – not by gang activity – but by long-standing loyalties to particular neighborhood blocks: Up the Hill; Down the Hill; Coppin Court. If asked, our young people would tell you that while this violence is partly tied to the business of drug-dealing necessitated by the absence of alternative employment (Cherry Hill's unemployment rate is nearly twenty percent), it's largely fueled by the perception that to be feared is to be respected. It appears from Southside students' accounts that the currency of fear is utilized evenly by Cherry Hill residents and the police officers who patrol through the streets. In Cherry Hill, says Aaron C., "no one can be sure who to trust."

We do not have solutions to the problem of violence in Cherry Hill, but we are convinced that our young people can help to lead us there. Just as teachers and parents need to develop strategies for listening regularly to urban youth, this must happen at the community level as well. What if our local radio stations routinely invited Baltimore City youth to speak out in regard to issues of concern to them? What if our television studios created a public access talk show hosted by Baltimore young people? What if the Southern Police District (located in Cherry Hill, a stone's throw from Southside Academy) established a Youth Council which met regularly with law enforcement officials who agreed to listen rather than preach? What if all of the adults in Baltimore took Lakeda's declaration seriously?

> If you want something to change just as
> well as they want something to change,
> you can put your thoughts and ideas
> together and you can have something.

What then Baltimore? What then?

References

Arrington, M.L. & Wilson, M.N. (2000). A re-examination of risk and resilience during adolescence: Incorporating culture and diversity. *Journal of Child and Family Studies, 9(2)*, pp. 221–230.

Cooley, C. H. (1902). *Human nature and the social order.* New York: Scribner's.

Erickson, E.H. (1968). *Identity: Youth and crisis.* New York: Norton.

Fenton, J. (2009, February 3). Teacher is called instigator of fight. *The Baltimore Sun*, p. A2.

Harter, S. (1990). Self and identity development. In S.S. Feldman and G.R. Elliott (Eds.), *At the threshold: The developing adolescent* (pp. 352-387). Cambridge, MA: Harvard University Press.

The future of publishing...today!

Apprentice House is the country's only campus-based, student-staffed book publishing company. Directed by professors and industry professionals, it is a nonprofit activity of the Communication Department at Loyola University in Maryland.

Using state-of-the-art technology and an experiential learning model of education, Apprentice House publishes books in untraditional ways. This dual responsibility as publishers and educators creates an unprecedented collaborative environment among faculty and students, while teaching tomorrow's editors, designers, and marketers.

Outside of class, progress on book projects is carried forth by the AH Book Publishing Club, a co-curricular campus organization supported by Loyola University's Office of Student Activities.

Student Project Team for *You're Not Listening:*
    Anika Gaither '10

Eclectic and provocative, Apprentice House titles intend to entertain as well as spark dialogue on a variety of topics. Financial contributions to sustain the press's work are welcomed. Contributions are tax deductible to the fullest extent allowed by the IRS.

To learn more about Apprentice House books or to obtain submission guidelines, please visit www.ApprenticeHouse.com.

Apprentice House
Communication Department
Loyola University in Maryland
4501 N. Charles Street
Baltimore, MD 21210
Ph: 410-617-5265 • Fax: 410-617-5040
info@apprenticehouse.com

www.ingramcontent.com/pod-product-compliance
Lightning Source LLC
LaVergne TN
LVHW051829080426
835512LV00018B/2790